To John,
Keep swinging for the fences! and keep shining your light! :)
Mary Rose Maguire

The Maverick Advisor:

The New Rules of Marketing for Financial Advisors and Consultants-Get Great Clients, More Respect, and the Fees You Deserve

Mary Rose Maguire

Copyright ©2020 by Mary Rose Maguire. All rights reserved.

This publication is licensed to the individual reader only. Duplication or distribution by any means, including email, disk, photocopy and recording, to a person other than the original purchaser is a violation of international copyright law.

Publisher: Mary Rose Maguire, www.maryrosemaguire.com

While they have made every effort to verify the information here, neither the author nor the publisher assumes any responsibility for errors in, omissions from or different interpretations of the subject matter. This information may be subject to varying laws and practices in different areas, states, and countries. The reader assumes all responsibility for use of the information.

The author and publisher shall in no event be held liable to any party for any damages arising directly or indirectly from any use of this material. Every effort has been made to accurately represent this product and its potential and there is no guarantee that you will earn any money using these techniques.

All rights reserved.

Table of Contents

Dedication	7
Preface	9
Introduction: Who Is The Maverick Advisor?	11
How It Used to Be...	14
How It Is Today...	15
How It Will Be Tomorrow...	17
Marketing: A Necessary Investment for Business Survival	19
The Maverick Advisor's Fast Intro to Marketing	23
Newsflash: Marketing Is Hard	24
Traditional Tactics	26
Digital tactics	28
The Maverick Advisor Rules	31
Chapter 1: Maverick Advisor Rule 1 - Use Direct Marketing	33
What If You Don't Market Your Business?	35
Marketing Is an Investment	36
Chapter 2: Maverick Advisor Rule 2—Develop A Brand	39
What is a brand? (More Than a Logo...)	40
Why Do You Need a Brand?	41

Table of Contents

How to Develop a Brand	44
Core Values	45
Strengths and Weaknesses	45
Unique Value Proposition	45
Personality and Image	46
Leadership Style	46
Relationship Style	47
Comparison	47
Different brand archetypes	47
Chapter 3: Maverick Advisor Rule 3 - Develop Your "Voice"	**51**
Why Developing Your Voice Is Necessary	52
How Developing a Voice Will Help You	53
A Strong Voice Qualifies/Disqualifies Prospects	54
Chapter 4: Maverick Advisor Rule 4—Always Use Your Voice	**57**
How to Use Your Voice on Your Website	60
Using Your Voice to Write Great Headlines for Your Website	61
How to Use Your Voice In Your Brochures	63
How to Use Your Voice In Your Ads	64
How to Use Your Voice in Your Emails	65
Chapter 5: Maverick Advisor Rule 5 -	
** Use Email Marketing Part 1**	**69**
Get Over Your Fears of Being Seen as a Spammer	69
Top of Mind Awareness Means Repetitive Messaging	71
You've got bread. Find the hungry.	72
How to Build a Fan Base	73
How to Choose an Email Service Provider (ESPs)	73
Lead Magnets	75
How to Promote Your Lead Magnet So It Catches Attention	77
Chapter 6: Maverick Advisor Rule 6 -	
** Email Marketing: Part 2**	**79**
The #1 Tip to Remember When Writing Email Messages	80
Autoresponders/Email Sequences	84

eNewsletters	87
Promotional Emails	88
New Launch of Services or Products	89
Reminders	90
Consistency... Consistency... Consistency: About Email Schedules	91
Chapter 7: Maverick Advisor Rule 7—Fire Up Your Marketing with These Service Packages	**93**
New and Improved	93
Version 2.0 and Beyond	94
QuickBooks Doctor	95
Tiered Package Offerings	95
Financial Advice	99
Membership Groups	100
Chapter 8: Maverick Advisor Rule 8: Use Direct Mail	**103**
Use Postcards for the Quick Win	104
Use Sales Letters for Telling a Bigger Story	105
"Shock and Awe" Packages	108
Chapter 9: Maverick Advisor Rule 9 - Test and Track	**111**
Frequently Test	112
Evaluate Results	113
Survey Clients	114
Chapter 10: Maverick Advisor Rule 10 - Research Your Audience	**117**
Client Surveys	120
Interviews	122
Afterword	**125**
Acknowledgements	**127**
About the Author	**131**

Dedication

To my smart and loving husband, Mickey, who believed from the very start that I was an author.

To my parents, Anthony, and Josephine, who encouraged me to read and reach for the stars. My life is brighter because of such love.

Preface

A passion for communication runs in my blood. You could say it is deeply embedded in my DNA. After all, my father was an extraordinarily successful manufacturers' sales rep and my mother was Italian. Both were skilled communicators.

So, it isn't a surprise I was drawn to marketing. Even as a young child, I was always searching for opportunities to share what I knew with others and to persuade them to take action. And an entrepreneur was born when as an eleven-year-old, I persuaded my parents to allow me to plan a neighborhood festival in our backyard to raise money for the Muscular Dystrophy Foundation.

With well-planned and thoughtful communication, great things can be accomplished. Throughout history, people have been motivated and inspired to achieve big goals when they understand a compelling message.

> *Wise men speak because they have something to say;*
> *Fools because they have to say something.* – Plato

I've been a marketer for over 30 years. During that time, I have seen companies make the same mistakes with their marketing. There often is a lack of understanding regarding 1) what business communication is and 2) how to communicate your expertise in an effective way.

To slightly revise Plato's quote, I'd say this:

> *Smart business owners speak to their target market's needs because they have something to say. Ignorant business owners speak mainly about themselves because they have to say something.*

Yes, lengthier than and perhaps not as profound as Plato's quote. But true, nonetheless. Communication is a two-way street. Often during conversation, a person will talk about themselves. Rarely do you meet people who will first ask you a question and then intently listen to your reply.

If you take anything away from this book, I hope it is a heightened awareness of communication and the part it plays in your business. Whether you see yourself in this light or not—you're in the business of communicating and persuading people to buy from you. Only after you've convinced someone to consider your products and services do you have an opportunity to close a deal.

I wrote this book to help those who want to improve their odds when it comes to increasing their sales and profit. I believe your success will rest upon effective communication and implementing it consistently in your own marketing. Once you learn the basics, you'll be flying with the eagles. How high is up to you. Let's soar together!

Mary Rose "Wildfire" Maguire
Columbus, Ohio
July 31, 2020

Remember to get your FREE book bonuses at www.TheMaverickAdvisor.com/bonuses

Introduction: Who Is The Maverick Advisor?

Like it or not, certain professions carry with them certain stereotypes. Doctors are perceived as having a superior attitude... lawyers are perceived as ruthless and cold-hearted... and advisors are perceived as boring.

It is true that many have a quieter, more introspective nature. But I've never equated it to being bland or boring.

I've written this book primarily for financial advisors but am including others under the "financial" umbrella. So whether you're a CPA, accountant, financial advisor, an EA, or a bookkeeper—the marketing advice contained within these pages will help you.

Advisors have survived up to this point by doing what they do best—helping individuals and businesses organize their finances and project the results of savings and investments so the person can see how well they are prepared for retirement.

They also help people make decisions with their money that will help them reach their financial goals as efficiently as possible.

When I use the term "Maverick Advisor," though, I'm not referring to the tasks you do. *I'm referring to how you market your business.*

Introduction: Who Is The Maverick Advisor?

The word "maverick" means an unorthodox or independently minded person, an individual who does not go along with a group or party.

That, my friend, is what you will need to succeed in the future when marketing your practice.

Realize I am going to be addressing a minority of financial advisor professionals with these ideas. Not all advisors are paying attention to the enormous changes that have occurred in their profession. They continue to think referrals will be the main way to get new clients and if they do a good job, those clients will remain with them.

What many practitioners don't realize (as well as other business owners), is your prospects and clients are getting slammed every day with alternative ways to spend their money. You may have a client today who is satisfied with you. But what if they get an irresistible offer from another financial advisory practice tomorrow? Why would that client remain with you?

This is where marketing comes into play. Marketing not only promotes your business to those who are unfamiliar with you—it also helps you keep the clients you already have and upgrade those current clients to new services.

Most financial advisory practices are considered small businesses. Quite a few haven't made their first $1 million in sales revenue. To be honest, those are the professionals I especially hope takes this book to heart.

There's a saying that goes like this: ***"What got you here won't get you there."***

In other words, everything you've learned about marketing your practice has allowed you to reach the current level you're at right now. But to move forward, you need to be open to doing things differently. Test new ideas. Try new things. Experiment and see what works.

Introduction: Who Is The Maverick Advisor?

That's how breakthroughs happen. It's only by dogged persistence and consistent effort you achieve anything of significance. The same dedication you applied toward getting your license and opening your business must also be applied to marketing. Below are ten wise "commandments" from the legendary marketer, Dan S. Kennedy–which is smart advice for you.

The 10 Traits of The Maverick Advisor:

1. Always uses an offer or offer(s) in their marketing material
2. Always gives a reason to respond right now
3. Gives clear instructions within their marketing
4. Relentlessly uses tracking, measurement, and accountability in their marketing
5. Uses only no-cost branding
6. Tirelessly pursues follow-up
7. Uses strong copy in all marketing material
8. Is not afraid of marketing that looks like mail-order advertising
9. Focuses on results. Period.
10. Understands that to grow their business, they must be a tough-minded disciplinarian and put their practice on a strict direct marketing diet.

So, did I scare away most of the room? Good.

If you're still reading and open to learning about marketing principles that work, then congratulations.

First, you *are* in the minority. And second, this means if you absorb the information in this book AND implement it rigorously in your practice, you'll not only stand out in the crowded marketplace, but you'll go far beyond your competition.

Before moving forward, we'll look at the advisor's relationship with marketing.

Introduction: Who Is The Maverick Advisor?

How It Used to Be...

It wasn't that long ago when advisors didn't have many options when it came to marketing their profession.

Attending networking events, joining community organizations, or simply talking to family members, friends, and neighbors was the extent of promoting one's practice. Many advisors today still think of advertising as a non-professional act.

However, as the old Bob Dylan song says, "...the times they are a-changing." Especially for accountants. Newer forms of digital marketing combined with the accountant's revised Code of Professional Ethics on March 31, 1978, demonstrates the need to take a closer look at advertising and marketing in order to ensure a practice remains viable in an ever-changing economic world.

Let me be clear: I am a passionate, unapologetic marketer. I realize not everyone will feel comfortable with some of the marketing tactics I consider a joy to test. At heart, I'm a risk-taker. I love to experiment with different methods, strategies, and ideas.

I also realize I'm a bit of an oddball for choosing to work with accounting, bookkeeping, and financial advisor professionals. Yes, I chose you. If you haven't thrown this book into the trashcan yet, then there's a chance you and I will become friends—if through these pages than nothing else.

You see, I'm on a search. A big search that has caused my loved ones to question my sanity... and the search is this: ***Are there advisors bold enough to understand the changes currently happening to their profession AND the magnificent opportunities they provide?***

You might be a practitioner who has been around for 25 years. Or you might be a brand-new owner who opened your practice three years ago. It doesn't matter to me how long you've been operating your own practice. All I ask for is an open mind to ideas and strategies which have the potential to increase your profits while building a stable practice.

If you're good with that, then I'm glad you're here. I have a lot to share.

How It Is Today...

Marketing is such a fast-moving target that if one had obtained a marketing degree just ten years ago, it would almost be obsolete.

Marketing technology is advancing quickly. The field, known as martech, has over 7,040 companies as of the writing of this book in 2020.

7,040.

Can you imagine the difficulty a Chief Marketing Officer faces when trying to choose marketing technology (martech) that will support his or her business initiatives? Additionally, all those software programs must play nicely with other programs—which often don't happen. What *does* happen are headaches.

I only mention this because it's important to realize if you're just starting to evaluate marketing activities for your practice, it's easy to quickly become overwhelmed. You're not imagining things. It *is* like the "Wild, Wild West" out there. It *is* difficult to gauge which software will live up to its promises and which would be a complete waste of money and resources.

I am not claiming martech doesn't work or it doesn't have a place in your marketing strategy. But what I am saying is you need to learn how to walk before you run. Many businesses try to dive into data analytics, for instance, before they even identify their marketing goals. And for some, they want to do this before even identifying their mission statement or the "why" they do what they do.

Today financial professionals can engage in more advertising, taking advantage of both online and offline marketing tactics.

But few do.

I write a lot of web copy for my clients. Home pages, Services pages, "About Us" pages, and more. Many businesses (including advisory firms), look at their website as a static brochure that simply lists how long they've been in business and their offerings.

If you're in this camp, realize you are severely limiting your earning potential.

Your website should not only engage your perfect prospect, it should present a clear path toward a specific, measurable action. Some examples of the type of action I'm referring to:

- Signing up for your monthly newsletter
- Filling a contact form for more information
- Downloading a special report
- Ordering a book
- Requesting a demo
- Registering for a webinar or conference

Your website offers you the opportunity to continually ask your visitor to do something. And you get to dictate what that "something" is—presumably choosing you as their solution-provider.

If only more business owners would realize they're in the driver's seat. **You** are the one who can create a clear path of action for your visitor. **You** are the one who can take the hand of your visitor and show them why you're the best choice for them.

Introduction: Who Is The Maverick Advisor?

You are the only one who can tell your story... the story that will engage a prospective client or customer and compel them to buy.

Which brings me to the message you'll hear throughout this book: You must differentiate your practice or you risk losing it.

Today, competition is more intense than ever. For instance, just a few decades ago, an accounting practice was competing against the other guy down the street. Now he's competing against "the other guy" across the country—and in some cases, overseas.

Because the competition has changed, your marketing strategy must also change. It's not enough anymore to attend a few networking events and talk about your business with a few trusted peers. The world has expanded with access to a multitude of choices for the consumer. The successful financial advisory practice in the new economy must adapt—or fade away.

How It Will Be Tomorrow...

I'm not a fortune-teller but I do keep up with the trends. And I can tell you the thriving advisory practice of the future will have invested time and money in getting their marketing strategy right.

Here is Merriam-Webster's definition of marketing:

> *The process or technique of promoting, selling, and distributing a product or service; an aggregate of functions involved in moving goods from producer to consumer*

Moving goods. I like the concept of movement because it implies action. That is what will be required from you to create a thriving, growing accounting practice. Deliberate, consistent, planned action.

Introduction: Who Is The Maverick Advisor?

As a firm owner in the future, you will need to understand:

- Why you do what you do
- What you do and for whom
- With whom you connect
- How to develop your story into marketing content
- How to use that content to generate sales

Content marketing is still considered a new development within marketing but has made big waves. Joe Pulizzi, founder of Content Marketing Institute (created in 2010), coined the name. His definition:

> **Content marketing is the marketing and business process for creating and distributing valuable and compelling content to attract, acquire, and engage a clearly defined and understood target audience—with the objective of driving profitable customer action.**
>
> *Epic Content Marketing: How to Tell a Different Story, Break Through the Clutter, and Win More Customers by Marketing Less: How to Tell a Different Story,* by Joe Pulizzi. McGraw-Hill Education 2014.

Businesses from pool companies to retail stores to high tech startups are all utilizing content marketing to engage their customers and clients and get new business. Fortune 100 companies now have entire departments dedicated to creating content for the Internet.

The future for financial advisory firms resides in how well—*and how consistently*—they create content that will meet the needs of their targeted audience.

If for instance, accounting practices all offer the same services, then how can they stand out from the competition? Why would a potential client choose you and not "the other guy" down the street (or across the country)?

Developing a unique marketing position will be an accounting practitioner's challenge. Understanding and leveraging various marketing tactics to promote their service will promote differentiation. This book is not going to cover every nuance of marketing. Data analytics, for instance, is a huge field. Technology is changing constantly. But this book will give you a foundation for marketing your business.

We'll tackle the many ways to differentiate your practice in the second section of the book, "The Maverick Advisor Rules."

Marketing: A Necessary Investment for Business Survival

I'll be honest. When I first told my husband I wanted to help advisors market their practice better, he was highly skeptical. So were a few of my business mentors. They all assured me advisors are highly frugal when it comes to investments.

However, I pressed on (and am pressing on by writing this book). I realize that investing in your business carries with it a certain risk. But I also have seen the competitive landscape change so drastically over the past twenty years that I didn't want to see financial advisors, bookkeepers, EAs, and accounting professionals left behind.

According to a 2014 study by the Association for Accounting Marketing, 30 firms were contacted to discover overall marketing spending (including compensation for marketing department) across their sample averaged 2.19% of firm revenue. On average, firms employed one full-time marketer for every 65 employees. Excluding marketing staff salaries, their top five spending categories were:

- Advertising
- Sponsorships
- Individual partner business development set asides
- Non-educational firm events
- Networking events/trade shows

However, there was a difference between what low-growth firms spent versus the marketing spend of high-growth firms.

- **High growth firms are actually spending less on marketing.** High growth firm marketing budgets accounted for just 1.04% of revenue (excluding compensation), compared with 2.08% in low growth firms.[1]
- **They are employing more marketing professionals.** They may be spending less, but they are prioritizing their marketing department at a ratio of 1:48 employees compared with 1:64. The right talent—and more of it—seems to be one way they're doing more with less.[1]
- **They are spending their budgets very differently.** High growth firms spent much more on their online presence, content and materials, networking and trade shows, and educational events.[1]

Most banking and financial firms will spend around 8% of their budget on marketing. Other businesses such as consumer services and tech software spend around 15%.

I would like to emphasize in this book I believe the best type of marketing is direct marketing. <u>Direct marketing is measurable</u>. According to Investopedia.com[2]:

> *Direct marketing is a form of advertising in which companies provide physical marketing materials to consumers to communicate information about a product or service. Direct marketing does not involve advertisements placed on the internet, on television or over the radio. Types of direct marketing materials include catalogs, mailers, and fliers.*

---

1 New Research on Marketing Budgets, Hinge Research https://hingemarketing.com/blog/story/new-research-on-cpa-marketing-budgets
2 Investopedia, Direct Marketing https://www.investopedia.com/terms/d/direct-marketing.asp

Introduction: Who Is The Maverick Advisor?

I know several direct marketers and copywriters who would disagree slightly with that definition. You *can* use direct marketing methods with television and radio. You just need a clearly stated offer with clear instructions to obtain an offer (which would include a way to track, measure, and achieve the end goal).

You would know, for instance, if you received any new business from a direct marketing mail campaign because there are specific measuring devices within such a campaign.

Compare that to attending networking events and trade shows and hoping for the best.

So yes, marketing is an investment and one you should take seriously if you want to grow your practice. But there are many options to consider. You want the biggest bang for your buck. During the rest of this book, we'll take a closer look at many of the marketing tactics that can grow your business.

The Maverick Advisor's Fast Intro to Marketing

If one obtained a marketing degree in 1988, a good portion of the education would be almost useless at this point. That's how much the field of marketing has changed over the past 30 years.

When I was in college, there was no Internet. Marketing consisted of the following channels: advertising done through television, radio, print, outdoor ads, telephone, and direct mail. A consumer's knowledge of a product or service was limited because the marketing channels were limited.

The traditional type of marketing was called "interruption marketing" because the advertiser was doing just that: interrupting someone as they focused on something else. So, a person was either reading the newspaper or watching TV and an ad would pop up. It was meant to switch the person's attention and initiate action.

Another type of marketing is "outbound marketing." Outbound marketing includes activities such as trade shows, seminar series and a sales representative cold calling prospective clients and customers. However, this type of marketing is costly. The return of investment (ROI) is dependent upon a lot of factors, some of which are out of your control.

For instance, you could invest thousands of dollars on a trade show booth. But if the promoters of the event didn't do a good job getting people to register, then all that money invested will have a lower ROI than if you had bought a mailing list of qualified prospects and directly mailed them a sales letter.

No matter what new technology has brought us over the past forty years, effective marketing has two components: strategy and tactics. You can't succeed with tactics if you lack a solid strategy.

Simply put, a marketing strategy is a plan for reaching a specific goal. A marketing tactic is the approach or tool you use to reach your goal. For instance, your strategy might be to increase sales by 20% in one year. One marketing tactic to achieve that goal could be creating a series of service packages which establishes your practice as an affordable choice or an elite one.

The tactics support the strategy. One of the biggest mistakes financial professionals make is defining the tactics before developing a clear strategy. As a wise man said, "When you don't know where you're going, any road will take you there."

Newsflash: Marketing Is Hard

If you're an accountant, financial advisor, EA, or bookkeeper and desire to grow your business, it is time to move forward with your marketing. You do it with written copy, video, or audio.

Work on your website and make sure it appeals to your target market. Meet prospects in person. Attend events and mingle. <u>The point is you are consistently moving.</u>

And you're *acting*. This takes a lot of time and effort. It's not easy. ***It's not supposed to be easy.*** If it were easy, everyone and your Aunt Sue would be doing it.

The point is, owning your own practice *is* hard work. And with marketing, you typically take two steps forward and one back. You try one thing... it goes over like a lead balloon and then you try something else. Maybe you keep doing this over and repeatedly. Until one day you have a breakthrough.

Which gives you enough air to keep going. This is the life of an accounting-related business owner. It is the life of **all** business owners. It is most definitely not for the faint-hearted. Here's my question to you:

How badly do you want it?

How badly do you want your practice to be successful? And if the answer is, "Bad... really bad..." then my next question is this: "What are you doing—**on a daily basis**—to get it?"

How much time are you willing to invest in your marketing?

For me, about 75% of my workday is hustling. *Not* writing client copy. Yes, I have client work, but I also am the sole marketer for Star Maker Marketing. This means all my marketing efforts are up to yours truly.

The blog posts, the LinkedIn articles, the tweets on Twitter, the updates on Facebook... Not to mention networking in my hometown and giving live presentations. Attending live conferences and webinars. I've been doing this for years. **Not months.** And I still feel like I have miles to go before feeling like I'm making a dent in the universe.

I'm not sure how much you've invested in yourself or your business, but **now is the time to take action.** Stop consuming information. Stop wondering if your word-of-mouth dreams are going to get you the results you want. Get out there and take a risk.

But remember... the action... the movement is entirely up to you. If you fritter away your day... your week... and only put in a half-hearted attempt to grow your accounting practice, guess what? You won't get far. But if you're willing to do the work, want success so badly you can taste it, then good. I want to hang with you.

I can be a "Dr. Phil" or an "Oprah." But right now, I'm "Dr. Phil." <u>Only you can be completely honest with yourself and know what's working—and what's not.</u> And just like Oprah says, you're only as good as your last show.

If you're not moving forward with your marketing in this hyper-competitive economy, then your competition has already left you breathing dust. Wouldn't you rather have your competition staring at the back wheels of your sleek Lexus as it goes screaming down the Big Profits Highway?

I thought so. Join me as we discover together ways to grow your business so you can enjoy the ride.

Traditional Tactics

I'll be honest. Although many marketers like to focus on digital marketing tactics, I still prefer the traditional approach.

And do you know why? Because they still work! I realize I've mentioned how much marketing has changed because of the Internet and consumer awareness. However, there are still some tactics that work just as well today as they did 50 years ago.

You might have been told that "direct mail is dead" or "no one reads a lengthy sales letter anymore." These are the same people who will tell you "social selling" is the new way to get attention from prospects and if you're not using social media in this way, you're missing out. I say rubbish. Direct mail is far from dead.

The Data and Marketing Association (DMA, formerly known as the Direct Marketing Association) has been tracking the response rates for direct mail over the past century. They were founded in 1917 and today's members represent some of the largest brands in the world—Google, Amazon, American Express, State Farm, Charles Schwab, and more.

Here are some statistics that proves direct mail has not only survived the digital age, but is thriving:

1. Direct mail household response rate is 5.1% (compared to .6% email, .6% paid search, .2 online display, .4% social media). This is the highest response rate the DMA has ever reported, since coming out with the Response Rate Report in 2003.[3]
2. Direct mail median household return on investment is 29% (compared to 124% email, 23% paid search, 16% online display, 30% social media).[3]
3. At 6.6%, oversized envelopes have the greatest household response rates over other mediums (followed by postcards at 5.7% and letter-sized envelopes at 4.3%).[3]
4. At 37%, oversized envelopes have the greatest household return on investment over other mediums (followed by postcards and letter-sized envelopes at 29%).[3]
5. The response rate for direct mail among people aged 18-21 years old is 12.4%.[3]
6. The top response rate tracking methods are online tracking such as Personalized URLs, otherwise known as PURLs* (61%), call center or telephone (53%), and code or coupon (42%).[3]
7. For every $167 spent of direct mail in the US, marketers sell $2095 in goods.[4]

---

3 DMA Response Rate Report https://thedma.org/
4 Print Is Big http://www.printisbig.com/
* PURLs are Personalized URLs. It's when you get a letter or postcard in the mail and it features a website address like this: www.greatcompany.com/MaryRoseMaguire.

Many would find it ironic, perhaps, that Google spends millions of dollars mailing promotional material to a consumer's home. And during the 2016 holiday quarter, Google more than doubled its TV ad spend, laying out $109.8 million for ads promoting its Google Pixel mobile device. Launching Google Home meant another $5 million for a single 30-second spot in January (www.responsemagazine.com, September 2017).

If an online giant like Google is still using traditional tactics such as direct mail and TV ads, there's an exceptionally good chance these marketing tactics aren't dead. Not by a long shot.

Traditional marketing tactics include direct mail, TV ads, radio ads, and print ads. Using these various mediums to communicate your message takes some planning, but the results can be worth it.

The important goal of using traditional tactics is to 1) understand exactly the type of audience you want to reach (industrial, high-net worth individuals, corporate, etc.) 2) create an irresistible offer and 3) use a good copywriter and designer to ensure your ad gets noticed.

Digital tactics

Digital tactics are an increasingly important part of developing an effective marketing strategy. Mobile advertising has recently surpassed desktop advertising—which means more and more consumers are checking their mobile phones for promotional emails and deals than they do on their desktop computers.

Mobile ad spend across all formats was expected to reach $98.3 billion in 2017, representing 23 percent of worldwide advertising expenditure, reported marketing intelligence service company WARC (https://www.responsemagazine.com, "Mobile Becomes Second-Largest Ad Medium, Overtaking Desktop," by Doug McPherson, December 6, 2017).

Marketers today face an incredible challenge, though, in keeping up with the thousands of marketing technology (martech) companies that are meant to help make data analytics easier. As I mentioned before, there are over 7,040 martech companies. These are "software as a service" (SaaS) companies that provide marketing services such as email marketing, customer relationship management, planning and management, business intelligence, website strategy and more.

Those are a lot of choices for a business to evaluate. And as I mentioned before, not all of them play well together, which causes unending headaches for a company's IT department. **So, I'm here to make things simple and easy for you: If you're just starting to learn about digital marketing, the most important tactic you can use is email marketing.**

Email marketing is one of the best ways to 1) control your own promotional outreach and 2) grow your business.

Online digital tactics also include digital ads, social media, online webinars, videos, podcasts, and online communities. However, with each of the tactics listed above, you are at the mercy of the platform owner. Many small businesses discovered the perils of depending on Facebook for their advertising when Facebook suddenly changed the rules. Whereas before a small business could promote their special offers on their Facebook fan page—they were shocked to discover Facebook had decided to only allow 1% - 2% of their "fans" to actually see their updates in their News Feed.

This is why I am relentless about email marketing. Once you build up your own list (and keep an Excel spreadsheet of the members' contact information), no matter what Facebook does (or Twitter, or Instagram, or LinkedIn, etc.), your list will be safe.

YOU will have control over connecting with your clients and prospects. You can do this through promotional emails, prospect emails, eNewsletters and more. Digital marketing is here to stay but you can still reap the benefits without getting overwhelmed. We'll explore email marketing in more detail in Chapter 6.

To summarize, yes—marketing has changed over the past 30 years. Digital marketing has allowed business owners to reach audiences more quickly than using traditional methods such as radio, TV, and print. However, using the traditional tactics of direct marketing is still effective. Print is still effective. Smart business owners today will use both online and offline tactics to increase sales.

What is direct marketing and how can you use it to your advantage? That's what we'll cover next.

The Maverick Advisor Rules

Maverick Advisor Rule 1 - Use Direct Marketing

What is direct marketing? I'll use the definition from the online site, Investopedia:

Direct marketing is an advertising strategy that relies on individual distribution of a sales pitch to potential customers. Mail, email, and texting are among the delivery systems used. It is called direct marketing because it generally eliminates the middleman such as advertising media.

Why advisors would love direct marketing: **Because it is measurable.**

Direct marketing consists of promotions – such as a direct mail sales letter, a postcard, a phone call, or an email – that solicit an immediate, measurable response from recipients. The key words are *immediate*, *measurable*, and *response*.

For example, look at the mail you received today in your mailbox. There's a good chance you received what often is called "junk mail." These are ads from businesses such as the local pizza parlor, an automotive repair shop, or the dry cleaners. If those advertising promotions use a direct marketing approach, you'll see there is a special offer for you if you use a certain coupon code or call a specific phone number and ask to speak with a person.

Chapter 1: Maverick Advisor Rule 1

Direct marketing isn't what's shown on most online business websites. For instance, open your Internet browser and search for a news channel. The home page will probably have a lot of banner ads. These ads will appear at the top of the page and often on the sides of a page. The large companies will often feature ads that look pretty but do not have a clear call to action. The response also cannot be accurately tracked.

This is why I'm not a fan of expensive Super Bowl ads. Companies spend a lot of money on the creative (an ad agency who handles the creation of the ad). There are countless meetings that occur, actors to hire, locations to scout for the filming of the commercial, scripts to vet, colors to choose, and more.

All this effort for what? So, everyone can talk about how funny your ad was the next day but when they're in the supermarket, buy the competitor's beer because it was on sale? To me this is a huge waste of resources. I much prefer the results gained from a good direct marketing campaign.

Direct marketing is... well, *direct*. It doesn't try to be clever or funny (sometimes humor is used, but it's not the focus). Direct response is developed for one reason and one reason only:

To get the consumer to respond *now* to the offer.

There is a proven formula for direct marketing. We'll discuss this in more detail in Chapters 8 and 9. This is why I love direct marketing so much. Because it works.

If you take anything away from this book, I hope you take away this: there are marketing tactics that have existed for a long time *precisely* because they give consistent, measurable results.

Direct marketing has been responsible for growing businesses into multi-million-dollar companies. It has made many business owners

Chapter 1: Maverick Advisor Rule 1

wealthy. Although some may think the approach is "old-fashioned" or not as hip as the trendier digital marketing tactics, believe me when I say direct response marketing is one of the best ways you can grow your business.

What If You Don't Market Your Business?

I often tell the story of my chiropractor. He was a fantastic chiropractor. Friendly. Competent. And most importantly, he helped alleviate the pain in my lower back.

"Dr. Jim" knew what I did for a living. I spoke to him several times about email marketing. However, he never scheduled a chat to discuss growing his business using the marketing tactics you'll learn about in this book. He also stopped attending the networking group where I originally met him.

I had many office visits in 2015 because of a back injury. In January 2016, I received a message from his office checking in. I didn't return the call because life got the better of me.

I then received an email in February and again, I didn't have a pressing need to visit Dr. Jim but put it in my "reminder" file. Then in April, I received an email that said Dr. Jim was closing the doors to his office for good. Every time I think of him, I get sad.

Because I know if he had consistently sent out helpful content to his patients that included special offers and reminders to schedule a visit, he'd most likely still have a thriving practice.

It's tempting to think of marketing your business as "optional." Especially if you're used to networking with others and getting clients through referrals.

I've seen some businesses make cuts to their marketing department when they needed to decrease their costs. But this is the worst decision a business owner could make. She or he is essentially stopping the one activity that would bring in more revenue to the business.

The consequences of not marketing are either lost client revenue or worse, a closure of the business. At the very least, you're leaving money on the table if you're not marketing your business on a consistent basis.

One of the most common mistakes professional service providers make is focusing so much on working *in* their business; they forget to work *on* their business.

For your business to succeed, you need to take the time to develop a marketing game plan. Without clearly defined goals and strategies to help you reach those goals, your business will stagnate and eventually die.

Marketing Is an Investment

Accounting practices are notorious for under-investing in their own marketing. They often fail to take their own advice which they give to their clients who own a business. According to a 2013 survey by *Accounting Today*, firms spent between 2% - 5% of their revenue on marketing.

The U.S. Small Business Administration recommends spending 7 to 8 percent of your gross revenue for marketing and advertising if you're doing less than **$5 million** a year in sales and your net profit margin — after all expenses — is in the 10 percent to 12 percent range. (U.S. Small Business Administration, January 9, 2013)

A 2016 survey of 168 Chief Marketing Officers revealed that marketing budgets account for as much as 40 percent of a firm's budget, with a median of 10 percent of the overall budget and a mean average of 12 percent. When shown as a percentage of overall revenue, the mean

Chapter 1: Maverick Advisor Rule 1

was 8 percent and the median was 5 percent. (CMO Survey Report, February 2016)

As you can see, most accounting firms spend less on their marketing than other comparable businesses. Since most accounting practices fall within the small business category, it's evident there is a lack of investment in this area. Other than looking at marketing as kissing your revenue dollars goodbye, let's consider another point of view.

First, as with any investment, you need to determine how to measure it so you get a healthy return. For those accounting firms who invest in marketing, the ROI is usually based on the first year's fee from a new client.

Say you want to secure ten new clients who are willing to pay an average fee of $2,000 per year. The marketing campaign requires an investment of $10,000.

On the surface, it might look like you won't break even. But if you instead consider that once you have a client, he or she will likely stay with you for at least seven years, the ROI increases considerably.

This describes a marketing principle called "Lifetime Customer Value" (LCV). It is the total revenue a customer will generate for a company. It may be expressed as total gross revenue or total net revenue.

In other words, that investment of $10,000 should be buying you fees of $140,000 over the course of seven years. So, the comparison isn't 2:1 ($20,000 of fees for an investment of $10,000) but 14:1! That's quite a return on a $10,000 investment.

The other point is when you develop a sound marketing strategy; you can re-use that same strategy year after year. Once you find the winning combination of marketing copy/design, the right audience, and the right offer—you can continue to run the same

Chapter 1: Maverick Advisor Rule 1

marketing campaign every year until it simply doesn't deliver results anymore.

Many businesses do this. They take the same promotional ad and run it in magazines for years. Or they run the same commercial for several years (a local beauty spa in my town ran the same Christmas radio ad for five years in a row).

When done right, marketing can be incredibly successful and provide lucrative results for your business. You only need to be open to test different approaches until you find the one that fits. You also need to consistently put forth the effort to do so.

One of my favorite sayings is the Latin phrase, *Audentes Fortuna Iuvat*. Fortune Favors the Bold. **In today's competitive, noisy marketplace, you must be bold.** You cannot wait for others to tell your story. **You need to be telling your own story to grow your business and you must tell it often.** Otherwise, be prepared to be swept up into the dustbin of oblivion.

Maverick Advisor Rule 2 - Develop A Brand

Many firms were founded by CPAs and financial advisors who were focused on building a solid book of business. Often, they used their last names as the name of the business. And many EAs and bookkeepers developed a client roster that depended solely on word-of-mouth.

But the last names of the founders are not a brand (or your last name). Not unless their mission and goals are crystal clear and are communicated consistently to their clients and prospects. This chapter will help you understand how to differentiate your practice from everyone else. A brand is your unique "calling card." It will let your clients and prospects know you offer remarkable services.

Your brand also is a way to build trust with your prospective buyer and your clients. When you consistently communicate a strong brand—demonstrating brand integrity—your audience will then know what to expect from you. This causes people to do business with you because they know, like, and trust you. Let's first take a look at what a brand is and why you need one.

Chapter 2: Maverick Advisor Rule 2

What is a brand? (More Than a Logo...)

An easy way to understand a brand is to study the brands that already have a strong following:

- The red Coca-Cola® logo
- The circles in the Audi logo
- The blue color of the luxury jewelry brand Tiffany & Co.
- The phrase "Just Do It" for Nike sporting goods
- The golden arches of McDonald's

Each one of these images or slogans represents a company that has spent millions of dollars to communicate a specific brand message. The brand message is how the company wants you to think and feel about them.

Coca-Cola® has trademarked their new slogan, "Taste the Feeling™." When you think of the beverage company, the images of pure refreshment and enjoyment come to mind.

When you see an Audi luxury automobile with the logo of intertwining circles, you're to think of connection and their slogan, ""Advancement through Technology." The company's name comes from the last name of founder August Horch. In German, Horch means "listen/hear." In Latin, "listen" is "Audi." It's not as straightforward as many brands but over the years, those circles have come to stand for quality and innovation.

The specific robin's egg blue color used for Tiffany & Co. is trademarked. This branded color has made a Tiffany & Co. gift box stand out from everyone else and immediately conveys elite status.

The branded phrase, "Just Do It" became the heart and soul of Nike's running shoes. The phrase immediately entered the public's mind and stood for perseverance, discipline, and determination. It became the rallying cry of those who wanted to win—both in sports and in life.

Chapter 2: Maverick Advisor Rule 2

The golden arches of McDonald's became synonymous with prepared food at an affordable price. That yellow symbol is now recognizable throughout the world.

Although each of the companies listed above have logos and colors to identify them, it is not the complete picture of a brand. For instance, Tiffany & Co. was founded in 1837 by Charles Lewis Tiffany and his friend, John B. Young.

Their store, located on Broadway, quickly became the go-to store for women who wanted to buy jewels and timepieces that had a clean, American style as opposed to the more ornate style usually associated with the Victorian era.

They only accepted cash for purchases in the beginning, never credit. And their focus was on the highest quality of jewels. Their company also became associated with love and romance, since many men quickly understood if they wanted to make a favorable impression upon a woman, giving her jewelry from Tiffany & Co. would do it.

Today, every woman recognizes the blue box that instantly conveys luxury and high-quality. A good brand is memorable and generates emotion. No matter what product or service is being sold, the successful companies connect their offering to an emotion.

Whether it's the determination to excel as an athlete (and be recognized) or the desire to be wealthy and successful—all the companies I've listed have found a way to make their customers feel important.

Why Do You Need a Brand?

There are many definitions for "brand," but I found a good one that keeps it simple:

Chapter 2: Maverick Advisor Rule 2

The marketing practice of creating a name, symbol or design that identifies and differentiates a product from other products. (https://www.entrepreneur.com/encyclopedia/branding)

The key word is *"differentiates."*

I've viewed hundreds of business websites and helped dozens of clients improve their website copy. However, there are some companies who look and sound the same. I came across this puzzling occurrence when I was a marketing manager for a cybersecurity company.

As I did competitive research, I quickly realized if I just switched out a company's brand and brand colors with another information security company—one wouldn't be able to tell the difference.

Unfortunately, the same can be said for financial firms. Many advisors have used the decades-long practice of naming their firm after the founding partners. "Smith, Smith, & James Advisors" doesn't say much in today's marketplace.

Law firms are the same. In fact, many professional services businesses lack any real marketing power and sustainability precisely because they've neglected creating a strong brand and promoting that brand with every client activity, they engage in.

However, I have particularly good news for you. There is still time for YOU to create something unique and memorable with your own practice. Believe me, you'd be in the minority if you did so (and thus, far ahead of your competition). But the Maverick Advisor understands he or she must do things differently to stay competitive.

Allow me to put it another way: Every accounting, financial advisor, EA, and bookkeeping practice offers basically the same type of services. From basic day-to-day bookkeeping, tax services, and auditing to retirement planning, management consulting, and fraud investigations. How does one firm differentiate their business from another one down the street? Why would a potential client choose your firm over someone else's?

Joe Pulizzi, founder of The Content Marketing Institute, said this (emphasis mine):

> Today, it is very hard to differentiate yourself according to products and services... because most companies offer the same thing. With today's technologies, anyone can copy what you create. **So the only way to differentiate yourself is how you communicate.** If we believe that's true, that means marketing must elevate itself in the organization and it becomes part of the broader business model. ("This Old Marketing" Podcast, Ep. 207)

The only way you can differentiate your services from another firm is to excel at communication. *This communication must be client-centric.* In other words, you need to understand your clients, what they really want (and it's not just financial advice), and then position your firm as the preferred solution.

Think of Apple computers and how they communicate their brand. There are many excellent computer companies that offer perhaps even better deals than an expensive MacBook Pro. But Apple has mastered the "hip, cool factor" of owning an Apple computer, which hits strongly the emotional trigger of wanting to belong to the "cool kids" group.

The same psychological aspect is in play with Starbucks. You can buy a cup of coffee at a local quick-mart, next to the gas station, but carrying around that cup doesn't convey the same impression as walking into the office building with the well-recognized white cup with the Starbucks green logo.

Chapter 2: Maverick Advisor Rule 2

I worked part-time at Starbucks just to learn how they delivered customer service. It was impressive, to say the least. There were weeks of training along with a thick employee manual which detailed how a Starbucks associate was to treat customers in addition to instructions for making the various coffee drinks. The goal was to deliver 'legendary customer service' so the customer enjoyed a positive experience (and would return for more).

Again—Starbucks is selling coffee. It's hard to think of a more commoditized item than a cup of coffee. So how did they become a multi-billion-dollar company? **By creating a strong brand that communicated exclusivity, luxury, and impeccable quality.** This is the kind of brand that is memorable and creates raving fans.

How to Develop a Brand

Now that you're more familiar with what a brand is, you may be wondering how to create one for your own business.

This takes some time and intentional thought. You'll need to find a quiet spot to work and bring a notebook and pen. It's time to brainstorm some ideas.

Consider these areas to identify your business:

- Core values
- Strengths and Weaknesses
- Unique Value Proposition
- Personality/Image
- Leadership style
- Relationship style
- Comparison to a well-understood person, place, or thing

Chapter 2: Maverick Advisor Rule 2

Core Values

The first area to tackle is your core values. Examples of a core values: integrity, trust, honesty, leadership, vision, thought leadership, innovation, respect, and competence.

Write down what you think your core values are. What would you like people to think of when they think of you?

Strengths and Weaknesses

Next, list your strengths and weaknesses. What do you excel at doing? What are your strongest skills? What is your expertise? What are the weaknesses that obstruct your growth?

Unique Value Proposition

Next, figure out your unique value proposition (UVP). A UVP, for instance, was Domino's Pizza "Hot, Fresh Pizza delivered to your door in 30 minutes or less... or it's free!"

Consider the promise you're making to your prospective client. What is the benefit they'd receive from doing business with you? For Domino's Pizza, they're promising to deliver a hot, fresh pizza within a short span of time. Then they cap off their promise with a guarantee (which is very powerful).

Your UVP needs to clearly state a promise, how it will benefit your client, and then to really clinch the deal... a guarantee. Include your unique expertise or the value you deliver that is different from another accounting firm or financial consultant/adviser. As an example, a CPA firm, Blumer CPAs, has as their UVP, "We proactively lead clients to equip them for growth."

There are several key words within that sentence. "Proactively" means they're taking charge and actively guiding their clients toward success.

"Lead" conveys authority and expertise. "Equip" is a great word to communicate a partnership and attitude of helpfulness. "Growth" is what every business ultimately wants because it will allow them to take on more business and be profitable.

Personality and Image

Next, take a good look at your personality. You might want to employ the help of those who know you best. Ask them how you come across. What are some of the words they use to describe you?

Maybe you're patient and deliberate. Or perhaps you have a great sense of humor that can encourage someone when they need it the most. An advisor who knows how to make people laugh… why not? Or you could be the strategic "Big Thinker" who helps people see possibilities they didn't consider before.

Write down all those traits. They'll come in handy as you develop your brand.

Leadership Style

Next, think about your leadership style. What kind of a leader are you?

Years ago, I was involved with life coaching. One of the questions a coach would ask a potential coaching client was this: "Do you prefer Oprah or Dr. Phil?"

Many women immediately recognize the difference. Oprah's style of communication is warm, inspirational, and encouraging. Dr. Phil's style is bold, blunt, and often confrontational.

Think of the leaders you admire and then consider your own style of leadership. Are there any similarities? If not, how are you different?

Relationship Style

Relationship style is another area that may require outside input. I'll use myself as an example for how to describe your relationship style: I'm open but deal in "black and white." I am diplomatic but do not shy away from telling the truth, even if it might be uncomfortable. I've been called honest and a "straight-shooter."

Ask those who know you best what it's like to engage with you professionally and socially. Are you easy-going or intense? Do you listen at great length before giving your response or can you read people quickly and in short order, sum up the issue they're talking about? A good description for that would be incisive or insightful.

Comparison

Finally, compare yourself to a person, place or thing that will allow someone to understand you better.

Example: "I'm like a trusted Sherpa who will guide you safely through the mountains."

Or, "I'm like a Swiss watch—dependable with interior processes that work seamlessly together."

Or, "I'm the Rolls Royce of advisors, delivering elite servicing with impeccable style."

Developing a brand is a lot of fun. Once you get a handle on what makes you different, you'll find marketing is a lot easier. You'll be able to capitalize on what makes you unique and truly stand out in an extremely competitive marketplace.

Different brand archetypes

What is a brand archetype?

Chapter 2: Maverick Advisor Rule 2

The concept of archetype comes from the psychology field—Carl Jung, to be precise.

A brand archetype is based upon symbolism. You're placing your brand in a very specific category or persona, anchoring your brand against something iconic—something already embedded within the conscious and subconscious of people's minds. For both the brand and the prospective buyer, it makes the brand easier to identify.

There are 12 basic brand archetypes:

- The Innocent
- The Sage
- The Explorer
- The Outlaw
- The Magician
- The Hero
- The Lover
- The Jester
- The Everyman
- The Caregiver
- The Ruler
- The Creator

One of my biggest frustrations is how often B2B companies want to be the "trusted adviser" (otherwise known as The Sage).

Once I gave a presentation to advisors where I touched upon this common occurrence. In fact, I told the room that they owned the brand archetype "trusted adviser." In fact, few other professions are trustworthy and competent as the accounting profession.

However, using the "trusted adviser" brand is not the only way to convey authority. In fact, in the pursuit of using this brand archetype, many businesses come across as stiff and unapproachable.

You know what I want to do with this pesky "trusted adviser" who keeps everyone enslaved to his boring ways? Throttle him. Now I know what you're thinking.

Chapter 2: Maverick Advisor Rule 2

"Hey, Mary Rose. Didn't you mention building trust is essential for an effective marketing strategy? Why all the hate for the trusted adviser?"

And you're right. I did say that. However, there a lot of ways to build trust. And really, it isn't just built with words. *It's built with action.* That's why I get slightly annoyed with the idea of "the trusted adviser."

It's as though accounting firms think if their marketing language can sound trustworthy, then **this is** what will position them as the best choice for their prospect. This reminds me of when I was a single lady and looking for decent men to date.

They weren't easy to find. I remember a guy friend giving me a great piece of advice.

"When it comes to trust, don't trust what a guy *says* he will do. Trust what he **does**."

A brilliant piece of advice I've since applied to different situations. Love. Business. Friendships. Partnerships. Everything. Words are important. But what is important is doing what you say you're going to do.

With digital marketing, there are some smart ways to build that trust. Sending emails on a regular basis is one way. Offering a monthly newsletter is another.

When your practice consistently "shows up"—whether on social media, with emails, in newsletters and brochures, even in a book— you're embedding the image of your brand in the mind of your audience.

B2B companies and professional services businesses have a wonderful opportunity to differentiate themselves further by choosing another brand archetype. Although it's important to be a trusted partner by your client, there are other brand archetypes you could choose that still would convey a sense of trustworthiness.

For instance, take The Creator. Those who have this brand archetype want to create things of enduring value. There is creativity and imagination involved but also a commitment toward excellence. People trust high-quality products and service. They realize they may have to pay more but are happy to do so if the value for their investment is clearly explained.

Think of the toy company, Lego, which is a good example of The Creator brand archetype. They want to help their customers build something fun and interesting by using their imagination. Lego, in turn, has carved out an exclusive spot in the highly competitive (and fickle) toy industry.

I also would like to add Lego published their own magazine for their fans. It ended in 2008 but a magazine called Lego Life is available in the UK and IE. They took the brand archetype and leveraged it into creating something extra they knew their fans would enjoy.

To learn more about brand archetypes, check out this SUCCESS Magazine article, "The 12 Brand Archetypes: Which One Are You?." Or you can contact me using the information given at the end of the book and I can send you the article through email.

Again, discovering your brand archetype will help you develop your "voice" when it comes to marketing your business.

What is "voice?" We'll explore it in the next chapter.

Maverick Advisor
Rule 3 - Develop Your "Voice"

Have you heard about the social media team at Wendy's, the fast-food restaurant? They're known for their quick-witted responses on Twitter, with a little attitude thrown in.

The restaurant chain has managed to communicate their mission statement (as of February 16, 2017: "To deliver superior quality products and services for our customers and communities through leadership, innovation and partnerships.") while keeping their customers—and detractors—entertained.

The superior quality products ("Always Fresh… Never Frozen" which describes their hamburgers), are promoted with a unique voice. So, what *exactly* is "voice" or "tone of voice?" **It's simply the personality of your brand.**

It could be irreverent and a bit rebellious (like Harley-Davidson) or imaginative (like The Walt Disney Company). It could be authoritative (like Charles Schwab & Co.) or playful (like Ben & Jerry's Ice Cream).

Your brand's voice will be directed by whatever brand archetype you choose. You wouldn't expect Harley-Davidson, for instance, to run a commercial which shows a man and a woman perfectly dressed in evening clothes, riding a motorcycle together while exchanging romantic, lingering looks with one another, right? Something would seem "off" about it.

That's because Harley-Davidson has already forged their brand archetype and voice. It's one of freedom and fighting authority. Breaking expectations. Living life by your own rules. Such a "voice" doesn't match a romantic image. This is what you need to think about as you create your own unique voice.

Why Developing Your Voice Is Necessary

Go to your computer and do a search for your "profession name + name of your city." Visit some of the websites. Now tell me, do any of them *sound different*? Look different? Or do most of them look and sound the same and have the exact same services?

Put yourself in the shoes of a business owner who is searching for a new professional service provider. What would cause her to stop in her tracks and say, "Whoa. They sound different. Who *are* they?" <u>That is why it's so critical to develop your own unique voice.</u>

I know what I'm proposing might sound completely alien to you. It might make you even feel a bit uncomfortable because after all, financial services is a "respectable" profession and you shouldn't have to be bothered with all this marketing mumbo-jumbo.

But trust me. Your prospective client is searching for this. They want to do business with an advisor who understands their needs but also realizes they have hidden desires, and they're yearning to do business with a company who "gets" them.

Years ago, a firm's competition was someone down the street. Now the competition is all throughout the country and even overseas.

Chapter 3: Maverick Advisor Rule 3

In addition, more technology has rendered many advisors' tasks as unnecessary.

Consumers have access to more financial information than ever. *But are they making the right choices with the information?* This, of course, is where you come in.

How Developing a Voice Will Help You

One of the most helpful decisions you can make to improve your marketing almost effortlessly is choosing a brand archetype and nailing down your voice. It will help you avoid a common mistake many business owners make (and a rather simple one to easily fix), which is *a lack of consistency.*

Consistency is the secret to effective marketing. No matter what you do, you need to give your marketing ideas a chance to breathe. Trying a method once or twice isn't going to get you the results you want. And effective marketing starts with being consistent with your brand's voice.

It's like developing a new relationship with someone you just met. If you met that person at a networking event and they were lighthearted, fun, and a true original—then met them for coffee and they were withdrawn, introspective, and serious—what would you think?

And if you saw this person's personality change drastically every time you connected; you might question the person's mental health. You know something's not right when a person is acting out of sorts. This is especially true if you know someone for a long time and then suddenly, they start to act "unlike themselves."

When you develop your own brand voice, you are demonstrating consistency and people trust consistent action. When you tell people what you're going to do—and then do it—it creates authority.

Take the time to develop your own voice and your prospects and clients will be appreciative. They'll know what to expect from you and in time, they'll trust you.

A Strong Voice Qualifies/Disqualifies Prospects

Communicating consistently a strong voice within your marketing not only builds trust, it will qualify (and disqualify) the type of clients you want to work with.

I know a copywriter who is deliberately abrasive. His "voice" is irreverent and a bit curmudgeonly. He even openly admits he hopes to discourage certain prospects from contacting him.

Every marketing piece he creates is written in this voice and clearly communicates the message that he isn't the type to coddle a client. He has a specific way of doing business and the groundwork is laid from his initial emails.

When you have a strong voice, it will be like a siren call to those who love that style and a bug repellant to those who are annoyed by such types. And that's what you want.

Why sift through prospects who "might" be a good fit (and turn out not to be) when your marketing copy can do it for you?

This is a great benefit from developing your voice. When you take the time to choose a specific brand archetype and create your own unique voice, you are essentially drawing a line in the sand. You are saying, "I want to work with people who understand what I'm saying… those who resonate with my message."

Chapter 3: Maverick Advisor Rule 3

And those who are attracted to such a voice realize you're the one they're looking for, the one who might finally understand their needs. It also allows them to get a taste of the type of business you run and prepares them for how you operate.

Create trust in your brand. Demonstrate consistency in your delivered service. Set clear expectations that are met.

It all leads to clients who know what they're getting, like what they're getting, and trust what they're getting. This leads to long-term relationships, repeat customers, and referrals.

Once you nail down your voice, what's next? How do you put all this great knowledge into action? This is the topic of the next chapter. Let's learn how it will work for you.

Maverick Advisor
Rule 4 - Always Use Your Voice

After you've identified your voice, it's time to let the world know about it! You want your voice to be heard in everything you create to promote your business. Your website, printed marketing assets, media ads, and emails.

But first, before we tackle all those different ways to "sing," I'll briefly address a common obstacle that prevents people from doing what I'm going to tell you to do.

I call it a case of **"What-If-itis."**

"What if my family sees this and jokes about it, doubting it will make a difference?"

"What if my competitor sees this and laughs, certain I've gone off my rocker?"

"What if I do this and end up turning off what could be one of the most lucrative clients I've ever had?"

Every person who has a creative bone in their body will understand this. It's called performance anxiety. It's the feeling actors, singers, dancers, and professional speakers get just before they step out on their platform.

They wonder if they're going to flop. They wonder if they'll remember all their lines. And they're worried they just may not be good enough. **You're good enough. Even brilliant.**

Throughout my life, I've not met many people who are "good with numbers." Most people are intimidated by numbers, let alone figuring out financial information. If you're able to wade through a stack of seemingly endless columns of numbers—and can give solid advice to someone about how they can save more money—then you're already a hero in my book (and a lot of other people's books).

CPAs, advisors, enrolled agents, and bookkeepers often don't receive the amount of respect they deserve. Other professional services such as doctors and lawyers usually don't face a high amount of resistance when it comes to their fees. But advisors are questioned all the time about theirs, as though they're gouging the client.

Therefore, you need to develop your own brand voice and promote it strongly. It is the key to differentiating your services from those who offer the same thing AND it will help prevent the "pushback" you receive for your fees.

Why does it work that way? I'll use Apple again as an example. It is debatable Apple computers are "the best." Their fans will make the claim (as will Apple) but many computer tech experts point to other products which are just as good or even better at a fraction of Apple's price.

The reason why Apple sells their products at a higher price is because they justified it with their marketing. It's really that simple.

Think about it. On January 22, 1984, during a break in the third quarter of the telecast of Super Bowl XVIII, a commercial appeared

Chapter 4: Maverick Advisor Rule 4

which made a huge splash. It was the now famous "1984" commercial by Apple, introducing their personal computer, the Apple Macintosh.

The commercial is a dystopian vision of a bleak future. The setting is an industrial complex, in drab, bluish tones, showing a line of people (all dressed the same, with shaved heads), marching in unison through a long tunnel toward an auditorium while a "Big Brother" image on a movie screen speaks to the audience:

> *Today, we celebrate the first glorious anniversary of the Information Purification Directives. We have created, for the first time in all history, a garden of pure ideology—where each worker may bloom, secure from the pests purveying contradictory truths. Our Unification of Thoughts is more powerful a weapon than any fleet or army on earth. We are one people, with one will, one resolve, one cause. Our enemies shall talk themselves to death, and we will bury them with their own confusion. We shall prevail!*

A nameless runner wearing a bright uniform of red athletic shorts and a white tank top rushes into the auditorium, carrying a large hammer. She's being chased by four police officers, who represent the "Thought Police." Undeterred, she twirls around and throws the hammer at the screen, releasing it as Big Brother announces, "We shall prevail!"

As the screen explodes amid bright light and smoke, the people watching the screen are shocked and seem to awaken from their stupor.

The commercial concludes with the narrator saying, "On January 24th, Apple Computer will introduce Macintosh. And you'll see why 1984 won't be like '1984.'" The screen fades to black as the voiceover ends, and the rainbow Apple logo appears.

A few important points: Not once did an Apple computer appear in the commercial. There wasn't anything said about the features and benefits of an Apple computer. No price was mentioned. And the ad was only shown *once* to a national audience. But the impact was enormous.

This ad positioned Apple to be a rebel, an alternative to IBM, a plucky underdog who sought to offer freedom from "groupthink."

Do you see how all those messages, sung in a unique "voice" was enough to get Americans talking about owning something that wasn't connected to IBM?

This is the power of voice. You can utilize it for your own practice. Let's look at how to make it work.

How to Use Your Voice on Your Website

Business websites now serve as the "welcome center" for prospects and current clients. But it isn't enough to simply welcome your website visitor. As Will Rogers said, "You never get a second chance to make a first impression."

Your business website must be ready to attract the exact type of client you want. I'll assume your website has a user-friendly design. But what about the website copy? One of the most common mistakes I see on a financial services website is a rather simple fix. When I visit a website, I often see either no headline on the page or a bland headline.

Let me use a familiar example for comparison: If you attend a lot of networking events, over the years, you likely have a pretty large collection of business cards. For many years, business cards served to help explain what a business did and some even included a few offers on the back of the card.

But once the Internet entered the scene, it was necessary to include the business' website address. And it is what people often check when they want to learn more about you.

Chapter 4: Maverick Advisor Rule 4

When you land on a webpage, one of the first things you do is look for a quick description of the website's mission. Ask if it speaks to you. You're tuning into the famous "WIIFM" Radio Station, which stands for: *What's In It For Me?*

You're asking the website: **do you have a solution for my problem?** Do you even know what my problem is and if so, how can you fix it?

Website visitors are busy. They don't have time to try to figure out what your mission statement is or what exact solution you provide for a problem they've got. Accountants, financial advisors, EAs, and bookkeepers have it easier than other types of businesses because their service is straightforward.

Everyone must pay taxes. And almost everyone works. There are many tax return services out there. How can you compete with H&R Block or Jackson Hewitt?

What you *don't* want to do is slap a cute or clever headline that really doesn't describe well what you do. Also, don't rely on cute photos (such as your dog or new baby) unless your target audience is veterinarians or pediatricians.

Using Your Voice to Write Great Headlines for Your Website

Your headline **MUST** have a benefit in it. It needs to speak to your target demographic, preferably with a solution to their problem.

What is the purpose of a good headline?

1. It is the bridge between your market and your product.
2. The headline does not sell: *Its job is to flag down your reader/prospect.*

Chapter 4: Maverick Advisor Rule 4

The job of the headline is **to get the reader to read the next sentence**... and the purpose of the first sentence is to get them to read the next one... and on and on.

There are four important qualities a good headline will possess:

1. **Self-interest:** An example would be "Lose 10 Pounds Before the New Year" Everyone would like to lose weight, so a headline like this would get attention.
2. **News:** An example of this type of headline would have words like "Introducing," "New!" or "Announcing."
3. **Curiosity:** A classic example of this headline: "How a Fool Stunt Made Me a Sales Rock Star." The headline appeals to the reader's sense of curiosity. They wonder what this "fool stunt" was and continued to read on.
4. **A Quick, Easy Way:** Everyone wants quick and easy. A good example of this type of headline would be: "Give Me Five Days and I'll Give You a Magnetic Personality" People respond well to quick and easy solutions.

One fail-safe way to make a good headline is to start it with "How To..." Starting your headline with "How To..." will force you to write copy that tells your reader how to do something, which is what your reader wants. People are interested in learning how to do things and with a "How To" headline, they'll immediately be attracted to it.

Your brand needs to be reflected in your website copy—in the headlines, the body copy, and even the "calls to action"—where you ask the website visitor to make a decision (either to call your office and schedule a free appointment, fill out a form for a free guide, or sign up to attend a free webinar, etc.).

Once you capture attention with your headlines, then continue to "sing" by highlighting how your services will help your clients.

Chapter 4: Maverick Advisor Rule 4

Always remember to focus on your client's needs first. Then you can explain later in your website copy how your firm can help them.

How to Use Your Voice In Your Brochures

Often, business owners do the same thing with their brochures as they do with their website. They only highlight themselves.

Too many companies use their brochure as a bragging arena. "We're The #1 Resource...," "We've Been In Business For 30 Years...," "Family Owned For 50 years."

However, you don't just start singing out in public without context. Although the "flash mobs" of random orchestra players in a crowded mall may generate excitement, that's not how it works with prospective clients.

You need to first get permission to sing. This means you must connect with your reader. And who does your reader really care about? You win the prize if you said, "they really only care about themselves."

Using the same principle as websites, including headlines on your brochures will let your prospect know you care about them. Your brochures need to first identify your reader's interests to build trust. Only after doing those things can you present your solutions with the expectation of being heard.

There are many copywriting formulas, but one of the most popular (and effective) is the PAS method. It stands for **P**roblem, **A**gitate, and **S**olve.

First identify a problem your prospect has. It could be a fear of overpaying in taxes. Or the frustration and difficulty involved with trying to figure out the new tax code.

After identifying the problem, you then agitate the problem by painting a noticeably clear picture of it and how it affects your prospect. For instance, a great headline is often a question, such as "Do You Dread Facing Those Complicated Tax Forms Yet Again... And Spending Your Entire Weekend Stressed Out?"

Listen, getting attention from your prospect is getting harder and harder every day. There are a ton of marketing messages he's receiving. There are hundreds of emails in his inbox, all vying for just a mere minute of his precious time.

That is why you must start taking your copy seriously. Both online and offline. Your brochures essentially have to grab your prospect from the collar, shake him hard and say, "Slow down! I know why you're having a hard time sleeping at night!"

Once you discover the real reason for your prospect's frustration/fear/anger/envy/sadness/shame and his desires—greed/revenge/happiness/health/love/passion/relaxation/freedom—then you can finally solve it. You position your services in the right light and sing "on key."

How to Use Your Voice In Your Ads

Ads still work. But the type of ads you run will make all the difference between them working "okay" versus *really* ringing your bell.

The problem with many ads (and the same can be said with online sites and brochures), is businesses will place too much emphasis on featuring an image. The image will often take up a lot of space. And that's valuable real estate—especially with an ad.

Again, remember an ad should focus on the prospective client. *Not* you or your business name, how many years you've been in business, awards you've won, etc. This means a photo of you should not be taking up half, 1/3 or even ¼ of the ad space. You need to stop muddying the water and diluting the purpose of running your ad.

The purpose of running your ad—and the ONLY reason you place an ad—is to get a prospect to contact you. You have your phone number prominently displayed, a website, address, and email address.

You need to have a strong USP (Unique Selling Proposition) in your ad. Put yourself in your prospect's shoes. She is likely asking this question: "Why should I do business with you rather than my brother-in-law's friend/business associate/H&R Block?"

A strong USP is like Domino Pizza's "Delivered in 30 Minutes... Or It's Free!"

What is yours? Do you have a guarantee regarding tax returns? A promise to reimburse in full any mistakes made that costs a client more money with their return? A free "money map" that shows them five hidden areas that could help them save money for their retirement?

The best way to generate leads with your ad is to offer your prospects something they want and make it easy and non-threatening for them to get it. Use your brand voice to communicate this message, but make sure you're delivering the type of message that will be heard—one focused exclusively on your prospect's interests and needs.

How to Use Your Voice in Your Emails

I have a saying: *"Bored gets ignored."* I can't tell you how many times I've received flat-out boring emails.

The subject lines are dull. The content isn't customized to who I am or worse, doesn't address my needs or interest. For the most part, many businesses just "phone it in" because sending email is so easy and inexpensive. Don't be like them.

Instead, you have an opportunity with email to truly stand apart from what everyone else is doing. Use your unique voice to communicate your services in a fun, interesting way.

Yes, I said "fun." And yes, you can include fun observations or views within an email that's about financial information. In fact, you can even show you take satisfaction in crushing the assumption "advisors are boring" (you know they're not, but it's a stereotype you can address with your marketing).

The most important thing to remember about email marketing is understanding the importance of your subject line.

Your email subject line acts as headline. It needs to persuade your reader to open the email and read the message. However, if the subject line is boring or doesn't bring with it a sense of urgency, it will often be deleted without a thought.

Once your email is opened, you must also immediately grab attention with your first sentence. We'll discuss more details about emails in the next chapter, but realize your prospective reader has dozens if not hundreds of emails she tries to process each day.

If your email isn't clear or doesn't get to the point quickly, guess what? It gets deleted quickly.

Therefore, you really can't lose when it comes to using your brand voice in your emails. It's also why it's so important and will set you apart from everyone else.

Just recently, I read the "About Page" of an accountant who has been in business for 40 years. He has a personal note on his page, and it opens with this, "I hope you forgive me for being blunt…"

Chapter 4: Maverick Advisor Rule 4

What a great introductory sentence! He does several things with this statement: 1) It takes on the stereotype of the accountant and slaps it around a little. 2) It's refreshing to hear someone be blunt because you know some honest truth-telling usually will follow. 3) And perhaps more importantly... it makes you CURIOUS. You want to know what he's going to be "blunt" about! What is it he's going to share that will help you?

All of those wrap up curiosity and self-interest with just a few short words, which is one of the most powerful types of headlines and introductory sentences you can write.

When you create your copy—whether it's web copy, brochure copy, email copy, any marketing copy—you must remember the reader is ONLY interested themselves and what will benefit them. This is why it's advantageous to use some creativity with your copy but at the same time, keep your focus on the other person.

How many emails do you get that don't even bring up a good point or raise an issue that urgently needs to be solved? I belong to a Facebook private marketing group and one time a web designer asked for feedback regarding his web page copy.

I gave him an idea he might not have thought about before. His current page focused on getting a website up and running for a low price. However, I told him I work with a lot of small business owners. And do you know what their real problem is?

Web designers who take too long to develop the site or worse, take the money and then completely disappear on them.

I've heard more "horror stories" about web designers than almost any other type of creative service provider. So, I told him he should emphasize on his website he was trustworthy and had a "system" or "process" that would notify a client where the project stood with a timeline.

I also suggested he gave a guarantee regarding how quickly he responded to client communication. All of this will help build trust.

How does this relate to emails? Simple. It helps you discover your prospect's real problem. It's often not quite what you think it might be. Then write emails that will address those problems in a compelling way.

If your brand archetype is the Magician, then write emails which address these problems with inspiring solutions. Include quotes from motivational leaders. Don't be afraid to use your imagination within the email message.

If your brand archetype is the Hero, then you want to save the world. Use inspiration to help move a person toward making the world a better place. You can use this by promoting a message which explains how saving money can help a person give more to those around them—their families, their communities, or their places of worship.

Email is cheap to send but avoid thinking it doesn't take some planning and effort. Once you get the hang of "singing in your voice," your clients and prospects will welcome your emails and even interact with you because of them. And isn't that the point?

In the next chapter, we're going to dive deeper into email marketing. This is one of my favorite marketing tactics. There is a lot to cover so buckle up!

Maverick Advisor Rule 5 - Use Email Marketing Part 1

When it comes to email marketing, you'll find plenty of online resources for strategy and tips on what to include in your messaging. But what you *may* not find is how to overcome mental obstacles so you can create an email marketing plan that delivers lead generation.

When I was talking about an email campaign with a business development manager, he was a bit hesitant. "I'm afraid if we send out too many emails, people will be turned off and will unsubscribe from our list. Won't we be a pest?"

Get Over Your Fears of Being Seen as a Spammer

If one issue concerns me with email marketing, it is this: a fear of being seeing as a spammer.

In fact, I had to break through this myself, which made me realize how often it holds people back and the consequences of giving in to this fear. No one wants to be a spammer, but let's look at the definition of a spam:

spam - noun *:unsolicited usually commercial e-mail sent to a large number of addresses*

Chapter 5: Maverick Advisor Rule 5

Another fun factoid: the meaning of the word originated from a skit on the British television series Monty Python's Flying Circus in which chanting of the word "spam" overrides the other dialogue (first known use: 1994)

If you've been involved with marketing, you know the perils of buying lists and then blasting emails to them (which can get you into a lot of trouble with email service providers). That's not how you build a list. You want people who show an interest in your business and sign up to receive emails from you.

In which case, those emails are *not* unsolicited. **People gave you permission to send them.** As far as "commercial" goes, there is a difference between sending a hyped-up email about a vitamin supplement and an email that delivers value to the recipient. Remember this word... **value**. We'll get to that in a minute.

Remember you're in business to help your target customers find a solution to their problem.

A story to illustrate this is the man who was fast asleep at night. Suddenly, he was awoken by a loud banging on his door. He tried to fall back asleep, but the banging continued. Finally, he got up to see who was at the door. It turned out it to be a neighbor who was letting him know his house was on fire.

Instantly, that neighbor went from being an annoying pest to a welcome guest! So, it is with your business. If you honestly believe your service or product will help your customer, then ***you need to let them know***. Email marketing is a great way to do this, but you have to get over the mindset you're somehow a "pest" when you let them know about your solution.

Will everyone see you as a solution? No. But you can't let the "not for me's" keep you from reaching the "yes for me's!"

Chapter 5: Maverick Advisor Rule 5

Don't allow your fear to keep you in the negative space. Realize there are plenty of people who need your help and the only way they'll learn about your solution is if you bring it to them.

Top of Mind Awareness Means Repetitive Messaging

There's a marketing term called "top of mind awareness" (TOMA). When your prospect is in the market to buy the type of service you offer, they'll think of your brand first. And why would they think of you first?

Is it because you send them a quarterly newsletter and then you're silent for the other eight months? (Hint: sending a message once every three months is not the answer.) Is it because you send one email newsletter a month? (Again, no.) Or is it because you send at least one email message a week, and if you're *really* breaking through your fear, more than one.

I have a copywriting guru I follow who sends me a promotional email every Tuesday and Friday. He sent me seven emails in November. Do I consider it spam? Of course not. I've bought one of his extremely helpful eBooks and most likely will buy more in the future. And the reason I do this (and enjoy his emails) is because **he brings me solutions**. He's a credible expert who delivers quality information I can use.

I didn't buy an eBook from him because of one email. I received several emails before finally seeing one which addressed a need. That's what TOMA can do.

My copywriting guru understands he is bringing value into my life. This is what you need to think about when you send your emails. Make them full of your expertise while focusing the message on your prospect's need.

Chapter 5: Maverick Advisor Rule 5

You've got bread. Find the hungry.

Craft your message in such a way to ***call out*** those who are hungry for your solution. Business owners are overwhelmed and confused by tax laws. Some business owners are clueless about bookkeeping. And many aren't sure if they'll be able to retire comfortably. They're unsure if they're making the right financial decisions for their business and their family. These types of concerns keep them up at night.

Hammer on their pain and then highlight your solution. Find ways to help them with their problem. Or use your authority to challenge the status quo. Send emails that address, for instance, new ways to save money. Everything from getting the best deal on office equipment to helping them find low-cost software.

Be helpful. I cannot stress this enough. Too many businesses send emails touting their services but fail to offer any helpful advice. Any knowledge you can share that can be implemented immediately will catapult you to TOMA status.

So, wrap your mind around what you can offer to those who need you most and go after your list with a passion!

Do not be afraid of being a pest. Do not be afraid of unsubscribes. It happens. Move forward to find those who *will* find your messages helpful and relevant.

Be bold. Be helpful. Keep sending your solution-centric emails to those who gave you permission to do so. The old sales adage says it takes 7-8 "touches" to reach a prospect. I have several friends who are sales professionals and they say the number has increased to 9-11! It has become even more challenging to capture a prospect's attention. Email marketing can quickly become your favorite way to get attention for your business.

Chapter 5: Maverick Advisor Rule 5

How to Build a Fan Base

Allow me to dispel a myth about email lists. You do not need to have a list of thousands to get results. All you need is a core group of clients and prospects who are engaged with your marketing message.

Some of the most powerful Internet marketers only have a list of around 1,000 names and many times, they get better results from their list than the guy with 20,000 names. So how does that work?

Look at building an email list as building your own "fan base." Just like a rock band has loyal fans that follow them throughout the country, you also can do the same. Create anticipation and yes, excitement, with your emails.

But before we get into the kind of emails you want to provide, let's first tackle the "nuts and bolts" of email marketing.

How to Choose an Email Service Provider (ESPs)

Every business owner has his or her own preferences when it comes to choosing the right email service provider. At the time of this writing, here are some of the current popular providers:

- AWeber
- Campaign Monitor
- Constant Contact
- ConvertKit
- Drip
- Emma
- GetResponse
- iContact
- Mad Mimi
- MailChimp
- SendGrid
- Zoho

Chapter 5: Maverick Advisor Rule 5

I've used MailChimp for over ten years now and highly recommend them. One reason I recommend them to those new to email marketing is because MailChimp offers a free version if you have up to 2,000 subscribers and send 12,000 emails or less per month.

They have beautiful templates you can customize easily, or you can create your own template. Their customer service is excellent and they're always trying to improve their service. Overall, I've been a happy customer and see no reason to switch.

However, there are larger software products that include email services such as Keap (formerly known as Infusionsoft). Those types of marketing automation products are rather overwhelming for someone who is just starting out with email marketing, so I often recommend a business owner first learn a simpler system and then, as the need for a more comprehensive solution develops—take a closer look at a product like Infusionsoft.

Bottom line: Using an email service provider will help you track your analytics. You'll quickly be able to see how popular a certain email was by viewing how many people opened the email and how many clicked the web links you included in the email.

This type of information will help you develop future content for your emails. Plus, you'll frequently get an email reply from someone if they have questions about the email you just sent. It makes it easy for your clients and prospects to stay in touch with you.

Use an ESP because you'll be able to integrate their opt-in form with your website, which is important for obtaining email addresses from your website visitors. Most ESPs make it easy to install their opt-in form on a website. MailChimp, for instance, provides the code to be added to a WordPress site. Or you could even grab their free plugin from WordPress' directory of plugins.

Chapter 5: Maverick Advisor Rule 5

This streamlines your process for getting email addresses. However, you need to have the right "bait" to entice someone to give you their email address. These "bait pieces" are often called lead magnets. Make sure you have at least one to get started. In time, you'll probably want to develop a series of lead magnets you can switch out on your website throughout the year.

Lead Magnets

So, what exactly is a lead magnet? A lead magnet accomplishes exactly what it says: it's a "magnet" to attract leads. Often B2B companies will offer a free report in exchange for a website visitor's contact information. Because white papers are one of the most complex marketing assets, often a company will ask for more than just a person's first name and email address on their opt-in form.

Some of the fields required to download a white paper: first name, last name, job title, company name, phone number, a question asking if the company is currently looking for a solution (with choices of 1-3 months, 3-6 months, 6-9 months, 9 months+), a question about what currently frustrates the person regarding the solution, and at times a comment section.

What else can you provide other than a white paper? Here are some ideas:

- Video
- Special Report
- Webinar
- Tip sheet
- eBook
- Free subscription (newsletters, video series, etc.)
- Podcast or recorded interview
- Assessment
- Coupon
- Discount
- Checklist
- Infographic
- Interview Transcript
- Free Trial
- Sample
- Exclusive Deal
- Quiz/test

Chapter 5: Maverick Advisor Rule 5

- Cheat sheet
- Case study
- Toolkit
- Sales material
- Free consultation
- A printed book
- Newsletter

You can also take a series of blog posts which cover a topic and create a special report or eBook from it. Another idea is taking a video or recorded interview, get it transcribed, and then offer it as a written document. You could even add the transcription as a bonus offer along with the video or audio MP3 file.

Your lead magnet should offer information to attract your target market. For instance, here are some sample titles to demonstrate this:

- *Straight Talk About Small Business Success in New Jersey* (target market: New Jersey small business owners)
- *5 Ways Boston Dental Practices Lose Money With Their Quarterly Taxes* (target market: Boston, Massachusetts dental practices)
- *What Most Cincinnati Trial Lawyers Miss With Cash Flow Management* (target market: Cincinnati, Ohio trial lawyers)
- *7 Tax Secrets the Most Successful Boise General Contractors Know And Use* (target market: Boise, Idaho contractors)
- *The 10 Biggest Bookkeeping Mistakes Restaurant Owners Make* (target market: restaurant owners)
- *How Philadelphia Small Business Owners Can Create a Robust Comprehensive Benefits Program Without Breaking the Bank* (target market: Philadelphia, Pennsylvania small business owners)

If you target a specific group of people—and channel traffic to your web page that features your lead magnet in a strategic way—you should receive a good amount of either hot or warm leads.

Chapter 5: Maverick Advisor Rule 5

How to Promote Your Lead Magnet So It Catches Attention

When channeling traffic to your web page, you can use both online and offline methods to get a potentially interested prospect to opt into your offer. Some of the most effective marketing campaigns use both, such as sending a mail piece directly to a list of potential leads with an offer for valuable information if they visit a particular web page (and have a simple website address in the mail piece, such as a sales letter or postcard).

You can also use the link to your web page that features your lead magnet in a variety of ways: include it in your email signature, on business cards, on the last slide if you give live presentations, as a "bonus" if people stay until the end for your webinar, or as a "giveaway" if you're a vendor at a trade show.

Really, anytime you can include a website URL and lead magnet offer, you should do so. If you use social media frequently, consider promoting your web page on an ongoing basis. Don't forget to use hashtags (the "#" sign) for your target market. Examples could be #CPA, #Tech, #SmallBiz, or #B2B.

Once you have a lead magnet on your website, you should promote it through multiple channels. If you use print advertising, make sure you offer it there (and add the specific URL address). If you do radio ads, mention the free lead magnet and direct people to the web page.

You can work with your web designer on creating simple website addresses for your lead magnet. The simpler, the better. You don't want to include a long website address full of random letters and numbers. Instead use something along the lines of

Chapter 5: Maverick Advisor Rule 5

www.smithcpas.com/FreeContractorReport or something along those lines.

Often people will jot down the address if they're hearing it from a radio ad so make it easy to remember. The same approach applies to anywhere you advertise your business. Simple gets remembered.

Remember to get your FREE book bonuses at www.TheMaverickAdvisor.com/bonuses, which includes an Email Campaign Tip Sheet!

Maverick Advisor Rule 6 - Email Marketing: Part 2

The reason I love email marketing so much is it allows a business to release "New Songs."

Remember the chapter on developing your brand voice? Sending emails on a regular basis gives you the opportunity to talk to your clients and prospects in that voice, further building trust in your knowledge and expertise.

Your emails allow you to build a relationship with your clients and prospects. The more authentic you are the better. Honesty and transparency are valuable currency. Too few businesses realize today's anxious world requires more effort than ever to gain the consumer's trust. The emergence of "fake news" and exposure of products and services that aren't living up to their claims only adds to the challenge that today's business owner face.

To cut through the skepticism and doubt, you need a channel which allows you to counter such attitudes with marketing that sounds different. And the quickest way to sound different is to say something provocative—but true.

When I say "provocative," I mean to tackle topics that might be what everyone else is saying but offer a different perspective. Challenge the status quo. Correct assumptions or misstatements. Such messages will continue to support your expert status.

The #1 Tip to Remember When Writing Email Messages

We live in an entertainment-saturated world.

This reality has affected every level of doing business. Many large Fortune 500 and Fortune 100 companies use entertainment in their ads. They also have developed their own content marketing departments, which regularly produce entertaining articles, videos, and podcasts.

So, it shouldn't surprise you when I say you need to use a few entertaining elements within your emails. Today's readers are overwhelmed with emails that are pure sales pitches. Very few of those emails are remotely interesting, let alone entertaining.

In fact, you want to create a blend of messages which are both educational and entertaining. These types of emails are commonly called "edutainment" emails.

Consider the type of entertainment you love best. Are you a jazz enthusiast? A huge comic-book movie aficionado? Never miss a gourmet cooking show on the Food Channel? Do you love salsa and Latin dance? Or maybe you enjoy author Michael Connolly's detective series?

Whatever you find entertaining, use some of this in your emails. As an example, here's one of my emails I sent on Memorial Day:

> **Subject line: By rights we shouldn't even be here**
>
> We're huge J.R.R. Tolkien fans.
>
> We've read *The Lord of the Rings*. We were mostly pleased with the film versions.

Chapter 6: Maverick Advisor Rule 6

There are a ton of great lessons in both the book and films, but one really touched me.

It touched a lot of people and today, on Memorial Day in the U.S., it seems appropriate to mention it.

For those who haven't seen the movie, here's the context:

An evil force called Sauron is trying to get back his power. Except he doesn't have his body (he's just this evil, flaming eye that sits on top of the Dark Tower).

And all this evil spirit needs for complete world domination is a special, magical golden ring.

The "One Ring to rule them all."

A band of good men (and hobbits, dwarves, and elves) get involved in the ultimate fight between good and evil.

The "One Ring" must be destroyed before evil Sauron discovers it.

So, two of the most unlikely characters find themselves tasked with this mission. Frodo and Sam. The hobbits.

The journey to get rid of this ring permanently (which can only happen by throwing it inside a volcano where it will melt away in the lava), is exceedingly difficult.

Too much to go into, but you need to read the book or at least watch the films to appreciate it.

So back to Sam's speech. It's a doozy. You'll be glad I set it up the way I did.

(You Tolkien fans already know where I'm going but isn't it fun to remember?)

So, Frodo is just plain worn out. He's beginning to think this quest of theirs is going to fail.

Chapter 6: Maverick Advisor Rule 6

He's ready to throw in the towel.

Call it a day and try to make it back alive to their cute little hobbit-holes.

Except Sam wasn't having it.

He gave one of the most inspirational speeches I've ever heard in a fantasy film... much less anywhere else.

Here's what he said:

"Frodo: I can't do this, Sam.

Sam: I know. It's all wrong. By rights we shouldn't even be here. But we are.

It's like in the great stories, Mr. Frodo. The ones that really mattered. Full of darkness and danger, they were. And sometimes you didn't want to know the end. Because how could the end be happy?

How could the world go back to the way it was when so much bad had happened? But in the end, it's only a passing thing, this shadow.

Even darkness must pass. A new day will come. And when the sun shines it will shine out the clearer. Those were the stories that stayed with you. That meant something, even if you were too small to understand why.

But I think, Mr. Frodo, I do understand. I know now. Folk in those stories had lots of chances of turning back, only they didn't.

They kept going.

Because they were holding on to something.

Frodo: What are we holding onto, Sam?

*Sam: That there's some good in this world, Mr. Frodo... **and it's worth fighting for.**"*

Chapter 6: Maverick Advisor Rule 6

On Memorial Day, we remember the veterans who fought for our freedom. Who gave their life defending what they believed in.

Because there is some good in this world and it's worth fighting for.

We'll always need guardians to protect what is precious. I am humbled and grateful we have so many who volunteer to do just that.

And may we never forget those who made the ultimate sacrifice.

We honor those lives today.

With gratitude,

Mary Rose

Now at the end of that email, I did mention my coaching services. However, the bulk of the email, as you can see, was spent on the "entertainment" portion.

I know this runs counter to the idea that in every email you must do straight selling. However, you'd be surprised how an email like the one above helps connect people to you. If the person shares the same interest, they bond a little more with you. Such "mini-commitments" add up when it comes time for someone to consider whether they should stay a client or not.

When I was writing daily emails, I used all sorts of entertainment references: Tolkien's "Lord of the Rings" films, Marvel's Comic Universe (Deadpool, Daredevil, Luke Cage, Captain America, etc.), Walt Disney, TV series (Once Upon a Time, Fringe, Halt and Catch Fire, Limitless, etc.), Michael Connolly's "Bosch" book series, and jazz music.

Chapter 6: Maverick Advisor Rule 6

Whatever interested me, I'd find a way to connect it to a marketing message. I know you can do the same thing with numbers and financial topics.

So, let's explore the different types emails you can send out to market your business:

Autoresponders/Email Sequences

Remember how we talked about lead magnets? And how you needed to connect your opt-in form on your website with your email service provider?

It's because you want to immediately start connecting with your new subscriber. Every email service provider has a feature called "autoresponders" or "sequences" (now, MailChimp has theirs under the category Campaigns/Ongoing).

This is a wonderful feature and I hope to help you take full advantage of it. Here's the idea: once someone signs up to receive your free downloadable report (or whatever you offer), they will then automatically receive a series of emails.

In other words, their subscription will trigger an automatic follow-up system!

Your follow-up system can consist of three emails sent over the course of one week or twelve emails sent within a 30-day timeframe. It's up to you. Generally, most companies will send a series of 3—7 emails over a two-week period. But again, it depends on what you want to communicate after someone signs up for your list.

Introductory emails are more important than you may think. In fact, research has found that welcome emails are read 42% more often than any promotional emails. As an email marketer, I can tell you anytime you have those percentage points; you'd be crazy not to leverage them. With a 42% more chance of connecting with your clients in a welcome message, you want to use that attention in the most strategic way possible.

On average, welcome emails receive an unusually high open rate of 50%-- making them **86% more effective than newsletters**. (source: Hubspot, "How to Plan & Execute Effective 'Welcome' Emails," https://blog.hubspot.com/marketing/plan-execute-welcome-email)

Your welcome email (sent right after someone signs up for your list) has a 50% chance of keeping your new subscriber reading your follow-up emails for the next 6 months! This is excellent news because the more emails they read, the more money they are likely to spend with you.

Therefore, you need to get your emails right from the very start. But it goes further than that. Research has also found reader response to welcome messages could give business owners greater insight into what their customers need and how their products or services can cater to that need.

A few "dos and don'ts":

Don't include images in your first emails (this includes logos in your signature area). Images often distract a reader's attention and can potentially cause your email to be marked as spam. For welcome emails, use only text for your message.

Do keep the text short. Short email messages (150 – 200 words) have a better chance at getting read. This is especially true for the first few emails you send. You are still building a relationship with your reader, so take it slow. You can send longer messages later (300 – 500+ words), after trust has been established.

Chapter 6: Maverick Advisor Rule 6

Do get to the point. Be clear about your purpose. If you want the reader to check out popular content on your site, quickly give them the links. Whatever your goal is for the email, reach it fast. Your reader will appreciate your direct approach.

Do provide a clear call to action. Keep it short and simple. Your readers need to know what you want them to do next. If your readers must guess, you'll probably lose them.

Examples of a call to action:

- Comment
- Share
- Read more content
- Visit a product or service page
- Subscribe to your email list (If the email sequence is sent to those who ordered an item but aren't on your list)
- Enquire about your product or service
- Join a community
- Watch a video
- A combination of the above

Do tell them what to expect from you next. This is vital to establishing a great relationship with your clients and prospects. They understand they're now on your email list, so let them know what to expect, and how it will help them. Essentially, you're training them to expect emails filled with great content and helpful information. This creates anticipation and will help increase your email open rates.

There are many ways to use autoresponder emails. Here are different reasons why you'd want to consider creating an autoresponder series:

- For follow-up after someone downloads your free report, watches a webinar, attends a live event, or visits your office
- To deliver an eCourse, which is educational content contained within the email itself (or the email contains a link to a webpage with the training material)

Chapter 6: Maverick Advisor Rule 6

- Re-activate clients who haven't purchased any service from you in months
- Remind prospects and clients about a service you provide
- Make a major announcement (with additional promotional copy) about a new development or special award you, your staff, or your office has won

Those are a few reasons to create an autoresponder series or email sequence. Envision your email as a news outlet, allowing you to publish your own press releases. Whatever you're doing that is new, noteworthy, or helpful—there's a good chance you can create an autoresponder series around it.

eNewsletters

eNewsletters are digital newsletters, sent through email. They often have a banner at the top which features the name of the newsletter and has images along with a few articles.

eNewsletters allow you to show more personality with your copy. The images also give you the opportunity to further connect with your reader with interesting graphics that captures attention. Your email service provider usually adds a link on the top of the email that gives the reader the option to read the eNewsletter in their browser. This is a nice feature for those who prefer to view a newsletter at a larger sized font.

eNewsletters are a great way to stay in touch with your clients and prospects. In fact, in 2014, I was able to track $10,821.34 in sales between Q2/13 to Q2/14 produced because of my eNewsletter. In fact, one customer told me that he wouldn't have thought to reach out again but then received my newsletter and remembered me. He ended up hiring me to do several more projects with him.

Keep eNewsletters entertaining and deliver valuable information. Be careful it's not too boring or "cut and dried." If your content is boring, you'll lose your reader—and future opportunities to connect. The next time he sees your email in his inbox, he'll likely delete it unless he knows there's something unique and interesting inside.

Promotional Emails

These are also called sales emails.

Promotional emails are exactly what they sound like—emails that promote your business. You could have a special offer you're running for a limited time just for your clients. Or you could send an email that asks a few questions with the intent of getting the reader to call your office and set up an appointment.

Promotional emails could contain news about your office, someone in your office, a new service, new rules, or regulations that will affect your clients, and reminders about upcoming deadlines.

You just want to remember to always include a strong call to action at the end of the email. Once you notify your reader, follow through by telling them exactly what they can do about the information they just read.

Promotional emails are a great way to market your business and generate excitement, anticipation, and interest. Here are a few tips for creating promotional emails that get results:

Always use a provocative email subject line. This is what will cause your reader to open your message. Use provocative statements, questions, and statements to arouse curiosity, specify results and stats, and customize email subject lines (Example: "John, are you ready to cash in on the tax changes?")

Use a headline in the body of the email copy. Yes, most emails start out with a "Dear Scott," or a "Hello." Some don't bother with a greeting.

But including a strong headline will help pull attention to the rest of your email. Get to the point as quickly as you can with the copy.

Test your email to make sure all the links work. Make sure to include a strong call to action at the end of your email. Even better: place a deadline or limited time offer that will further encourage your reader to act quickly.

Keep track of your email list, those who open the emails and the links they click. **If you find that someone is opening a lot of your emails and engaging with them**—*and this is a person who hasn't been contacted for some time*—**go ahead and use this as a good reason to call them.** Emails can create opportunities so don't miss them.

New Launch of Services or Products

Whenever you offer something new, you make sure it's announced throughout your marketing assets. This means your announcement should be featured within your monthly newsletter and in your emails.

Announcements should also be included in:

- A new brochure and/or sell sheet
- On your website
- On social media

Also, remember to put out a press release and send it to news outlets. Don't just limit it to your own local city. Use online press release distribution sites like PRWeb and PR Newswire to ensure your press release is seen by national news outlets as well as your local area. Don't forget to send an email to your list with a link to your press release.

Do you know that financial advisory clients often leave their current provider for another simply because they want a specific service which they think you don't provide?

This is why it's important to make announcements and promote them on different channels. Check to ensure your current clients and prospects know you've unveiled something new.

The problem with clients leaving is unless you have an unhappy customer who acts, you don't know they're gone… until long after they're gone.

Very few customers and clients will tell you why they left. They just leave. This usually leaves you scratching your head while mumbling, "Was it something I said?"

Well, it might have been something you said. Or something you didn't do.

Therefore, it's so important to constantly promote your current services and new ones. Email marketing makes it easy to do this on an ongoing basis. All you need is a little planning. Take the time to sit down and list all your services on one document (if you've not done this already). Then look at the calendar and plan to emphasize at least one of those services for one month.

When you launch a new service, also make sure to build up some excitement. Send out emails which essentially say, "We have a big announcement in March… you won't want to miss it!" weeks before you make your big announcement. Arouse people's curiosity about what you're up to and give them teasers to stoke their interest.

Reminders

I appreciate reminders from the businesses I work with. With accounting services, you already have a built-in reason for reminders—the taxes are due! And with financial planning, everyone knows that someday they'll likely want to retire and enjoy life.

Email is a wonderful tool to send out those reminders. Most of the time, people are busy, and an important deadline date can easily be overlooked or forgotten. You can further strengthen your role as a "trusted adviser" by sending a friendly reminder to your clients about an important upcoming date.

Also, many accounting and bookkeeping offices will have special hours from February—April. And if you're really rocking your marketing, you might even have an exclusive "Platinum Level" type of service only available to a small group of your best clients. Not only send email reminders to them but mail them directly with the information.

A side note: if you've developed tiered pricing, always mention you'll be sending something separate to the highest level of membership. Treat your clients as members of an exclusive club and you'll be able to command higher prices for your services.

People like to belong to something. It hits a deep need within every human being. If you create experiences within your practice meeting that need, you'll be much more successful than a financial advisor, accountant, EA, or bookkeeper who doesn't (and who mistakenly thinks that after April 15 is gone, they should be, too).

Consistency... Consistency... Consistency: About Email Schedules

Every time I talk about marketing, I talk about consistency. Consistent marketing action is what will bring you results. I remember a conversation I had with the owner of one of our favorite Asian restaurants.

"Andrew, have you ever tried radio advertising?" I asked.

The reason I asked was because I looked around at a nearly empty restaurant during dinner time and thought it was a shame. His food was good, and the prices were reasonable. The restaurant was clean and had a nice ambiance. His answer almost made me choke. "Sure," he said. "I tried radio advertising. Once."

Once won't cut it. Especially today when we have constant marketing noise. You're not just competing with other accounting, financial advisors, and bookkeeping practices for business. You're competing with Amazon's online advertising, Walmart's television advertising, and the hundreds of other businesses who are running ads in newspapers and magazines.

In other words, other businesses are out there consistently promoting their message. You must do the same. I tell my clients to run a marketing strategy for at least six months. This usually gives you enough data to determine if the marketing is successful or not.

With email marketing, you need to be consistent with your schedule. If you're sending an eNewsletter, let your subscriber list know they can expect it on the second Wednesday of the month (or whenever you want to publish it). Then follow through by keeping that schedule.

When you state how often you will send emails to your list, it not only prepares your subscribers, but it adds to your credibility when you make good on your promise.

You probably won't see results right away when you start using email marketing. But in time—and with the right messages—you will get a response. However, it all hinges on you being consistent with your efforts.

Remember to get your FREE book bonuses at www.TheMaverickAdvisor.com/bonuses. Discover how to build your email list with one of the bonuses: a webinar on using landing pages and squeeze pages to generate leads and increase sales!

Maverick Advisor Rule 7 - Fire Up Your Marketing with These Service Packages

Apple comes out with a new, updated version of their products every year. They also highlight why the newer version is better and much preferable than the current one you might own.

I've always been fascinated with the excitement and anticipation that typically follows a "new product" announcement from Apple. And then I thought about B2B companies and professional services. Why don't more businesses create their own "Big Announcement" party?

Why, indeed. I realize it sounds odd ("You can't buy our service from a Walmart aisle..."). I understand the product or service isn't the same. Yet I'd like to bring up an important point: people are used to looking for "new and improved."

New and Improved

Like it or not, the buying public has been trained to pay attention to new products and services. Companies like Proctor & Gamble have targeted women for decades on "new and improved" laundry detergent, toothpaste, and shampoo.

Chapter 7: Maverick Advisor Rule 7

Browse any grocery store aisle and you'll see several packages with "new and improved" on their label. And... they get bought. So why can't you do the same?

The truth is, you can—**and should**. You should plan to roll out something new at least once a year. When you do, promote your new service in several ways (press releases, brochures, newsletters). Sending a big announcement through email is another effective way to do it.

In fact, I'll even nudge you at this point to consider a "launch party." Why not? You would be the first advisor, accountant, EA, or bookkeeper in town known as "The Party Advisor" or "The Party Bookkeeper!" Of course, you'd need to do several launch parties to earn that nickname, but if you do it right, people will remember you. And being remembered is a crucial outcome of good marketing.

Version 2.0 and Beyond

I use the WordPress content management system as the platform for my website. As of this writing, I'm using version 4.9.8. Realize there was a 4.9.3, 4.9.2, 4.9.1, etc. preceding the most recent change. Software companies feature their new versions of "2.0 and beyond" to improve usability and add new features.

Like the "new and improved" approach toward packaging your services, you may want to consider marketing one of your strongest services but position it as a "Version 2.0." You don't have to develop something new. You can easily take some of the services you already provide and combine them into a new offering. You can also add "bonuses" or certain services to make your "new and improved" offering even better.

When you announce your new version, make sure to let your clients and customers know you've listened to their requests and developed the new version to make things easier, more efficient, more economical, etc. The bonus is that your clients will understand you are always working hard to create better services for them—which creates more loyalty and customer lifetime value.

QuickBooks Doctor

I've seen several accounting practices offer this and it's one of my favorite types of services. It's so important to offer your clients a service that will help de-mystify a system.

In this case, QuickBooks is used by many individuals and small business owners. However, these same clients make a lot of mistakes with using QuickBooks (which ends up becoming "SlowBooks" for you as you try to untangle the mess). Use terms such as "doctor," "scientist," or "repair shop" to instantly explain that your service will fix something.

I also would include a few diagnostic checklists to your marketing mix. Offering a quick and easy way for a client to assess their situation (and determine that they need your help) would be extremely beneficial for both you and your client.

Feature such checklists or questionnaires on your website. For added punch, offer them as a free download for those visiting your website. You can then follow up with them specifically with more questions regarding their use of a system and market your services in a targeted way.

Tiered Package Offerings

Today you see tiered package offerings with most online "Software as a Service" (SaaS) companies. They usually offer three options: the basic, the most comprehensive, and the one in-between (often called "Our Most Popular Choice.")

Chapter 7: Maverick Advisor Rule 7

There is, as you might have imagined, a science behind this. Marketers will test the positioning of such options, switching out prices, the size and color of fonts, specific language, and more. To put it simply, people like choices. And they usually like to see what types of features are available to them for a specific price.

Most people will tend to go to the middle. They want something more than something basic yet they don't want to invest in the ultimate choice. However, remember there are people who always want the best and to them, that means buying the most expensive option.

You can be creative with the naming of your offerings. Popular names are:

- Silver, Gold, Platinum
- Essentials, Deluxe, Ultimate
- Beginner, Advanced, Expert
- Individual, Small Business, Enterprise

When designing these packages, realize all the "extras" you can offer. For instance:

- More face-to-face meetings
- Availability after work hours
- Access to a private online portal
- Membership site
- Customized reports both printed and sent as a PDF
- A visit to a business owner's location for a "Lunch and Learn" session on finances
- A workbook that includes specific directions for completing a financial task
- An annual special dinner when your client can "ask you anything"

Really, there is almost no limit to the various add-ons you could offer to sweeten the deal. And if you offer any of the above already (and

Chapter 7: Maverick Advisor Rule 7

you're not marketing it as anything special)—**STOP!** I know this might not sit right with you but indulge me.

The most important asset you have is your time. The second most important asset is your knowledge. For many years, advisors have given away both – often without fair compensation. I love advisors. I have rarely met one I didn't instantly like.

It's because advisors are overall good people who genuinely want to help others make better use of their money. Frequently, this trait allows others to take advantage of their time and expertise. As a result, many advisors run into the problem of not being valued and receiving push-back regarding their fees.

People push back because they don't **understand** the value you bring to them. Therefore, tiered pricing can be advantageous. A tiered pricing table clearly spells out for your clients and prospects exactly what you *do* offer and what the person will receive when they hire you.

I have a story regarding the type of people who always want the best. It has to do with one of the most common automobile items: tires.

Sure, you can buy the Nitto Invo Luxury Sport Radial Tire for just $370 a pop. I mean, it's okay for *most* cars. But what about a tire encrusted in **gold and diamonds?** Now *that's* elite!

In 2016, a company in Dubai (where else?) produced their first set of tires with 24-carat gold leaf and embedded diamonds. Each tire featured the sparkling stones in the firm's logo. Gold leaf was placed around the edges in a checker pattern.

They were first designed in Dubai, and then transported to Italy, where an artisan jeweler decorated the tires with diamonds. Then, the four tires were shipped back to Dubai where gold leaf was applied by the same guy who worked on Abu Dhabi's presidential palace. The price? A mere $600,000.

I mean, really... who *wouldn't* want to pay half a million for a set of diamond and gold tires? The luxury tire company donated the money to the Zenises Foundation, which focuses on improving access to education around the globe (a lovely gesture).

The moral of this story is that if you create something elite – something most people wouldn't want or couldn't afford – you can be sure SOMEONE will buy it if you position it right. *And if it's marketed to the right audience.* Dubai is known for its outlandish extravagance. University parking lots are filled with six-figure cars. They'll gold-plate just about anything over there.

How can you use this information for tiered pricing? Pull a Neiman-Marcus. The high-end retail store Neiman-Marcus puts out a Christmas Catalog every year, filled with luxury gifts. They also include items only a billionaire could afford.

Do many people order these over-the-top expensive gifts? No. But it only takes one half-million-dollar sale to make it worth Neiman-Marcus' time to include it in their selection of gifts.

One such item from their 2017 Christmas Catalog was His & Hers Rolls Royce Limited Edition Dawn Coupes ($439,625 and $445,750 respectively). I have no doubt someone bought those as a treat for themselves and a loved one.

Or do what Starbucks used to do. Starbucks sells gallons of coffee which cost pennies to make yet they charge dollars. However, when they had an online store, they also sold a $1,295 Nuova Simonelli® professional-grade espresso coffee machine on their site. Believe me, *someone* bought those machines.

Chapter 7: Maverick Advisor Rule 7

If you don't have a "luxury model" of whatever you offer, why not? Those who have the money to buy expensive items buy them because they *can*. It's a psychological thrill for them. And you might be missing out on all the fun.

What's *really* a kick is writing copy for these items. *Performance... commercial-grade components... professional... ease and style...* This is the kind of copy that makes even the biggest coffee snob drool with anticipation.

This is why you want to plan on offering an ultimate, elite, and "everything-and-the-kitchen-sink" type of service for your tiered package. Not only does it appeal to the high-value client who can afford it—it also serves as motivation for those in the middle. If they put in some effort, they also could reach the exclusive level. There is a lot of psychology attached to pricing and product positioning. Tiered packages are one way to tap into it and generate more revenue for your business.

Financial Advice

I have spoken with several advisors who have told me they offer financial advice all the time—and often without any type of compensation.

I also realize many times, advisors may feel as though they don't get the same type of respect as doctors and lawyers, even though they, too, offer an unbelievably valuable service. However, my brother is a lawyer and he charges a pretty penny for his time. If someone wants to find out if they have a legal reason to hire him, he will meet with them and briefly assess the need.

But after determining that, he goes into "pay me" mode. He doesn't offer free legal advice, much less details for any "do-it-yourself" solution (although such solutions are limited within the law profession).

Chapter 7: Maverick Advisor Rule 7

Compare this approach with many advisors. For instance, today the accounting profession is changing at a fast rate and many tasks which before were handled by junior staff are now achieved with software programs and artificial intelligence products.

This is why the President and CEO of the American Institute of Certified Public Advisors (AICPA) Barry C. Melancon, Accountant, CGMA, strongly urged advisors to move into becoming more of a financial advisor during his keynote address on "The State of the Profession" at the 2017 Digital Accountant Conference, held in San Francisco by AICPA technology subsidiary CPA.com.

Mr. Melancon pointed out advisors need to learn new skills, but also unlearn old ways of thinking. Firm models will need to change, both internally—how many entry-level to more experienced staff to have on your team—and externally—how you manage your relationships with clients. He mentioned he has seen more firms experimenting with subscription-based relationships, where for a flat monthly fee; the outside accountant takes care of all a client's accounting needs.

He also mentioned the enormous recent above-trend growth in technology-enabled client advisory services as a great example of the kind of higher-end offerings advisors can deliver. Again, this is an area that advisors can add to the specialized and more robust tiered packages.

Financial advice is valuable to your clients. If positioned in the right light and supported with strong marketing messages, your clients will also see the value and realize how important it is to invest in their financial future.

Membership Groups

This is a marketing concept that few advisors are using to grow their practice. Membership groups can be a way to entice new clients and create curiosity and anticipation with your current clients.

Chapter 7: Maverick Advisor Rule 7

What is a membership group? It's really nothing more than a private group you control. You set the guidelines for who belongs to the group and you enforce access to the group in a consistent way. Businesses that have a membership group often choose others as administrators to help run the membership group.

For instance, you could use a membership group as a bonus for clients who sign up for the most expensive service in your tiered pricing table. The membership group could be used as another way to deliver value to your clients.

A good marketing "rule of thumb" is this: the more access a client has to you, the higher the fee you should charge. Many accounting and bookkeeping practice owners have others perform the bulk of servicing the client. However, there are other clients who for various reasons, place them in a different category (such as long-term clients or business clients who are in the top 10% for yearly revenue).

In that case, treat your best clients in a special way that demonstrates how much you appreciate their business. No matter how long a client has been with you, showing appreciation in tangible ways will always be appreciated.

Here are some ideas for where to host your membership group.

Offline (meeting times could be once a month or once a quarter):

- Local restaurants
- Local colleges
- Chambers of Commerce meeting rooms
- Corporate or small business meeting rooms
- Hotels
- Libraries
- Whole Foods

Chapter 7: Maverick Advisor Rule 7

Online:

- A private portal to your website
- A private Facebook group
- A LinkedIn Group
- A membership forum
- Meetup.com: it offers a way to connect with people online and allows you to send invites for live meetings in your area

The important point is to set a calendar for events and create an agenda. If you have an online membership site, respond quickly to comments and questions. Ask for input and feedback from your members. Have those who are administrators or moderators actively oversee the group and keep you informed if you're unable to participate on a regular basis.

With a little effort, your membership group could go a long way toward deepening your client's loyalty to your business. A membership group also allows you to distribute marketing information such as newsletters, recorded interviews, videos, and more to give your clients helpful content they can use.

Maverick Advisor
Rule 8 - Use Direct Mail

With all the activity and attention digital marketing gets, who thinks about "snail mail?" Newsflash: Direct mail still works. In fact, you might be surprised how many Fortune 500, Fortune 100 and Fortune 50 companies rely on direct mail for their marketing.

Direct mail still gets the best response when it comes to earning attention from clients and prospects. Although email marketing is popular, the strongest open rate typically hovers around 20% for business and finance according to MailChimp's statistics (https://mailchimp.com/resources/research/email-marketing-benchmarks/).

If you're not using direct mail to reach out to your clients and prospects, then hopefully this chapter will encourage you to do so.

For instance, not all your prospects are sitting in front of a computer all day. Using email marketing is important but put yourself in your client or prospect's shoes. Are they checking email constantly throughout the day? Or putting out fires? Or perhaps they're busy dealing with their own customers and clients? At any rate, their attention is selective and limited. Often, the one sure-fire way to get through to them is with a good old-fashioned sales letter.

Chapter 8: Maverick Advisor Rule 8

To further illustrate this, I recently spoke to an accountant who wanted more contractors, electricians, and plumbers as clients. I immediately asked him if he was using direct mail to reach out to these prospects. He admitted he was not. I told him such jobs aren't "desk jobs" and because of that, his best chance to reach them would be with a postcard or sales letter. There are more details to this strategy, which I'll explain next.

Use Postcards for the Quick Win

Postcards are a wonderful way to get your message across to busy people. First, it's hard to ignore the message of a postcard. It's right there... out in the open! Immediately your recipient can see the marketing message.

Second, it's more economical to send a postcard. At the time of this writing, a postcard costs 35 cents to mail versus 50 cents to mail a First-Class letter. If your postcard is not larger than 4¼" × 6" (but at least 3½" × 5") you can mail them at the 35 cents rate.

Here are a few "Dos" and "Don'ts" when using a postcard to get new clients:

- Do use a powerful headline to grab attention
- Do make an offer very clearly
- Do give your prospect a reason to respond right now
- Do make sure you have a good tracking system in place, so you know a prospect came from your postcard campaign
- Do feature strong copy on the postcard
- Don't use large images that take up too much space (the space should be filled with great copy, instead!)
- Do use several ways to contact you (phone number, website address)
- If you are sending your prospect to an online website address, do use a URL link shortener like www.bit.ly. Make your URL link short and easy to remember.
- Do include your return address

Chapter 8: Maverick Advisor Rule 8

Remember to also send more than one postcard if you choose this method. Sending just one postcard won't get the same response as sending it to the same people two more times. Again, people are busy, and it takes several attempts to reach them before gaining their attention.

Use Sales Letters for Telling a Bigger Story

Because a sales letter has more space than a postcard, it allows you more room to make your offer. Your sales letter could be just one sheet of paper or several. If you do create more than two pages, though, you might want to consider having the sales letter printed on a 11"x17" piece of paper and then folded to fit inside the envelope. The entire sales letter will then be kept together.

There are more comprehensive guides out there that will tell you exactly what you should include in a sales letter. I highly recommend the book, *The Ultimate Sales Letter: Attract New Customers. Boost your Sales*, by Dan S. Kennedy. In it he gives examples of a successful sales letter.

The purpose of a sales letter is to sell your services to someone. Nothing less. Follow the same "Dos" and "Don'ts" I listed before for postcards (except for space limitations). Make sure you use a headline, though, for your sales letter. Headlines are vital to capture attention quickly and prepare your reader for the rest of your letter's content.

Whatever your offer might be, realize there will be objections. Imagine your client or prospect reading your letter while saying, "So what?" The statement, "so what," is an objection to overcome. Remember that for each claim you make, you must back it up with proof.

The proof could be statistics, results one business or client received, current trends, industry news—any credible information you can pull in to prove your claim. A good sales letter sets up the reason for the letter (presenting the PAS formula explained in Chapter Five, which is Problem, Agitate, Solve).

Begin by addressing the pain your reader is experiencing or ask a question that assumes the pain. Identify the problem clearly within the headline and the beginning of the letter.

Next, "agitate" the pain by further "dimensionalizing" it. Dimensionalizing is when you paint a picture of how frustrating/challenging/scary, etc. it is to have the problem. Once you establish the pain, then you can present the solution—but not before.

The biggest mistake most business owners make with their sales letters is they don't take enough time to demonstrate to their reader that they understand them. Your reader is smart. He isn't going to pay attention to a pure sales pitch. Instead, you need to carefully bring him onboard by proving you know how tough things are for him.

This is the part of a sales letter where you are establishing trust. Once a client or prospect knows you "get them," they will be much more agreeable to hearing your offer.

For an even better response, add a reply card with a stamp on it. These can be quite simple. On one side, have your address (for even better tracking, use a code at the bottom of the card to let you know the reply card came from a specific direct mail campaign).

On the other side, feature an area for qualifying questions, such as the example below:

Chapter 8: Maverick Advisor Rule 8

Smith & Johnson Advisors: (Choose the most appropriate option below)

[ ] Please contact me to schedule a free consultation call with you.

[ ] Give me a call ASAP. I have an immediate financial advisory need in mind.

[ ] Not interested right now. Try us again in _____

Name _____ Title _____

Company _____ Phone _____

Address _____

City _____ State _____ Zip _____

My business is: _____

Type of financial help I need: _____

[ ] Taxes and Financial Planning   [ ] Financial Advice

[ ] Forensic Auditing   [ ] Assurance Services

[ ] Payroll   [ ] Bookkeeping

[ ] Information Technology Services   [ ] International Accounting

[ ] Environmental Accounting   [ ] Other _____

Sales letters can be one of the most effective ways to grow your business. It is said the formula for success goes like this:

- 40% of your focus should be on the offer
- 40% of your focus should be on the mailing list
- 20% for everything else (copy and design)

I've seen some great sales letters fail because it wasn't mailed to the right list. Or it failed because it had a weak offer.

Just like postcards, you need to mail more than once. Plan on mailing at least three sales letters to the same group of people over the course of 30—45 days. After sending the first letter, the second letter should be sent 8—10 days later. The third sales letter should then be mailed within 8—10 days. This is designed to get the fastest response.

Another approach is to mail three sales letters over the course of two months (or 60 days). After mailing the first letter, you'd mail the second letter around three weeks later. The third sales letter would then be mailed after another three weeks.

The power of sequence cannot be overestimated. Your clients and prospects usually will need to hear from you *consistently* before acting.

"Shock and Awe" Packages

If you really want to impress someone, consider sending a "shock and awe" package. They are larger in size and contain several items, so they will be more expensive to put together. However, it is an excellent way to gain attention. No one can resist opening a large package or bulky mailer. They are curious about its content. This is especially true if your package feels heavy.

What goes into a "shock and awe" package? You can include a variety of items depending on whether your package is for lead generation or part of a new client welcome package. If you're trying to sell your services to a new prospect, you'll need marketing assets such as sales brochures and testimonials.

If it's to welcome a new client, you'll need items that further support your expertise and credibility like a book and onboarding material. It's also a nice touch to add branded marketing items such as coffee cups with your logo, a calendar, pens, or a USB flash drive. Check out promotional marketing companies for ideas.

Chapter 8: Maverick Advisor Rule 8

By the way, branded promotional items are a great way to support your marketing efforts. You want your clients and prospects to think of you every time they use your cup, a calendar, pen, or anything else you sent.

Include as many items and diverse items as you can. You want your recipient to feel as though they're opening a gift, with enjoyable surprises added into the mix. Also break up material into different, smaller pieces. For instance, instead of putting a checklist within a printed workbook, consider making the checklist into a laminated bookmark.

Although you want the items to be business-oriented, it's a nice touch to throw in fun surprises like the branded items (a keychain, a mini-journal, a nice checkbook cover) and even some edible treats like fancy chocolates or gourmet coffee. You want the person receiving the package to feel like there's a lot going on with the contents.

As an example of a "Shock and Awe" package that would go to accounting prospects may include items like this:

- Screenshots of tables, charts, etc. that show how much money was saved during the year or quarter (with private information blurred out)
- DVD with video testimonials from happy clients
- A booklet explaining ways to get the biggest deductions during tax season
- A booklet(s) on new services and options from new tax laws, especially if the tax law specifically targets businesses you serve
- A checkbook cover, monthly expenditure log, calculator
- A coffee mug with the firm's brand and inside, individual packets of gourmet coffee, tea, and hot chocolate, or an edible treat
- A coaster branded with the logo and tagline of the firm
- A book authored by the owner or a series of leadership articles by him or her
- All packed into a reusable money box

Chapter 8: Maverick Advisor Rule 8

Does this sound like a lot of stuff? Yes, it does! And that's the point. Think of how you'd feel if you received a small package with a promotional pen and a sales letter from a business. It's nice but doesn't really leave much of an impression.

An example of a smaller Shock and Awe package that serves as a welcome package to new accounting clients might include these items:

- Any educational materials broken into manuals, CDs, DVDs, etc.
- A notepad to take notes while watching the DVDs
- A coaster to hold a cup of coffee while watching the DVDs
- Other relevant goodies (for example, include a calculator with courses on investing, or a pedometer with a diet/exercise program)

As you have probably figured out by now, many of the gifts are cleverly designed promotional materials. Compare receiving just a letter with a few inserts to receiving a medium-sized box that has been carefully packaged and you open it to reveal around 7—9 items. It makes a MUCH bigger impression and the person can't help but feel special from such preferential treatment.

The person realizes you probably don't send such a package lightly, but they were someone who ranked high enough on your list to get one. There are many psychological triggers with this marketing tactic. The goal is to get the recipient to respond and the "Shock and Awe" packages practically guarantee your business will get noticed and receive a response.

Maverick Advisor
Rule 9 - Test and Track

If a business is weak in marketing (aside from first, doing it at all), it would be in the testing and tracking area. Larger companies have a marketing team where several staff members are devoted to this function. As an accountant, financial advisor, EA, or bookkeeper, you know the value and importance of tracking numbers. Within marketing, measurement is also vital to know what's working—or not.

When I was in college, I switched my major to marketing. I lasted one semester. The one class which tripped me up was quantitative analytics. In the 1980's, it was done with spreadsheets and human calculation. Today we have software that automatically tracks everything from buyer behavior to complex predictive analysis. Technology has made this vital aspect of marketing so much easier.

The good news is that not only has the software gotten better (and more granular), but it's completing these tasks faster than ever before. The bad news is as a result, many marketers are now overwhelmed by data, forced to sift through an endless mountain of reports while neglecting to focus on developing marketing strategies that work. Discovering the "happy medium" of getting enough data and the right data—is today's marketing challenge.

Chapter 9: Maverick Advisor Rule 9

As you probably can imagine, a little information can go a long way. However, this should tell you there is ample information available that will let you know how well your marketing is performing.

Frequently Test

When copywriters write a sales letter, a business will usually send out a "test letter" to a small section of their mailing list. Typically, you want to send a test mailing to no more than 20% to 25% of the total mailing list.

When it comes to online testing, it's a little easier. First, you can quickly see results. Second, you can also change elements of your marketing quickly (depending upon having a responsive web designer).

Here are some potential areas to test for your marketing strategy:

- The colors on your website
- The colors of your call to action buttons
- The headline on your website pages
- The title of your "free download" eBook, report, etc.
- The introduction copy for your home page
- The copy of your website
- The length of copy for your website
- Images
- The call to action

Split testing, or A/B testing is when you create two of the same offer but you use different elements with each. For instance, on one web page, you may use "Save Big With Your Taxes This Year!" and on the other web page, have this headline, "New Jersey Business Owners Agree: Smith & Johnson Helped Them Grow."

Your website developer can help you create different web pages, or you could use a landing page service such as Leadpages. Or if you use a marketing automation platform like Hubspot, ActiveCampaign or Mailchimp, they also allow you to create different landing pages.

An important distinction: when testing for direct mail, often several elements are tested. However, when you test your digital marketing (your website, email, and any online content), only test one thing when doing an A/B test.

For some of these changes, you may see an immediate result. Others may take a few months before seeing a difference. Monitor your efforts as closely as you can to determine which approach is the winner.

Evaluate Results

When you test various types of changes, carefully look at the results. Did that new headline on your website perform better than the previous one? Did blue test better than orange? Or maybe you tested an offer with a rock-solid guarantee.

Whichever is the "winner," you then want to apply the results to the rest of your marketing. Consider using the more successful headline as a headline for a postcard campaign. Or use the more popular color for other elements for your marketing material (brochures, business cards, newsletters, etc.)

Software companies also can give you results, such as Google Analytics (which analyzes your website for visitors, most popular posts and pages, the demographics of your visitors, and more). Leadpages, a software-as-a-service company, offers landing page templates for your website. They will provide a click-through rate for the landing pages, allowing you to see which ones are performing well and which ones may need some adjustment.

Here are some other tools to help you evaluate results:

- Hotjar—an all-in-one analytics and feedback software service
- CrazyEgg—provides snapshots of your website visitors and tracks their activity path
- Lucky Orange—an all-in-one conversion optimization software suite

A conversion is when someone responds directly to an option. It could be a "Join Today" button on your website, to encourage a website visitor to sign up for your newsletter—or it could be a "Call Today" message within a sales letter you mail to a list of prospects.

For instance, when a website isn't converting website visitors into newsletter subscribers, the marketing team goes to work to figure out how to fix it. There are a variety of ways to address the issue. Some of the more common ways to improve conversions include changing:

- The copy – is it too long? Too short? Too vague? Doesn't address the problem or create a sense of urgency?
- The call to action – is it bland? Unclear? Uninteresting?
- Design – would a red button work better instead of green? Does the font size need to increase? Are there images needed? Are there different images you could use?

Tracking your results will help you get the most out of your website. Very often, visitors don't do what you think they will do (or what you want them to do). Using such tools as those listed above will help you connect with visitor preferences so you can improve the usefulness of your website.

Survey Clients

One of the most important ways you can improve your marketing is by surveying your current clients. Asking for feedback can give you crucial insights that can make a huge difference in your marketing strategy.

Chapter 9: Maverick Advisor Rule 9

Make it easy for your clients to give you feedback. Place contact information on all of your client communication assets including your email signature line. Ask for feedback on a regular basis. You can use online surveys to collect information.

If you want more insight regarding a specific service, choose a small sample of clients who are using that service and create a short questionnaire for them to complete. Some possible questions to ask:

- Why did you choose this service?
- What has been the most valuable benefit of this service?
- What surprised you about this service?
- What frustrated you about this service?
- If you could wave a magic wand over this service so that it was perfect, what would it look like?
- Would you refer others to this service? Why or why not?
- Did this service meet your expectations? If not, what disappointed you?
- If you could, would you choose this service again?

You want your clients to be as truthful as possible, even if hearing the truth might sting a bit. Often, you learn more from the complaints than the praise.

If you survey your clients on a regular basis, you'll find the results will keep you on track for marketing success. It is true you can't please everyone, but over time, you'll notice response patterns. If, for instance, a dozen people complain the new website re-design isn't working for them, you can ask them more questions about what they find difficult.

By asking for genuine feedback, you accomplish two things: 1) your clients will see you care and 2) the feedback will act as a roadmap for creating a more effective marketing strategy. We'll be diving deeper into client surveys in the next chapter.

Maverick Advisor Rule 10 - Research Your Audience

A successful copywriter once shared with me an interesting anecdote when he hung out with some of the top copywriters in the country. Copywriters have their own "inside baseball" language like any other profession. They also love to talk about various methods to persuade someone to buy.

So when a group of copywriters get together, it's easy to think their conversation will revolve around whatever the newest marketing tactic is working well or if they tested their copy with a new online software program that generates more leads.

However, this successful copywriter said those topics were not what these copywriting giants talked about. Instead, the *true* "hot topic" was a question they would ask each other: "What to do you know about this particular demographic my client is trying to reach?"

In other words, what captivated these successful copywriters *weren't* methods or software. What was important was *targeting audience intelligence.*

Many businesses start out with focusing on their product or service. They seek to improve their solutions, however—they often forget to check in with their target market. Ask yourself these three key questions:

First—is there a real need for what you're selling? What may sound like a great idea to you won't matter if there is no demand for it. Don't offer answers to questions no one is asking. Do your due diligence before marketing a product or service. Make sure it meets a real need.

Second—is there competition? Competition is a good thing. Few things are harder than bringing to market an unknown entity you must explain to a potential buyer. As someone wise said, pioneers often die with arrows in their back. You don't have to be the first. Just differentiate your solution with your own creativity and resourcefulness.

Third—have you surveyed your prospective audience to find out as much as you can about them? I can't stress this enough. If you don't survey your market, how will you know what to say to them? If you don't know their pain points, their frustrations, and insecurities, then it will be difficult to create a marketing message that will attract them.

If you ask any marketer worth their salt, they'll agree knowing your audience inside and out is the key to effective sales and marketing. For instance, if you're targeting contractors, you need the demographics (age, gender, marital status, educational level, etc.) and psychographics (hobbies, magazines they read, TV shows they watch, music preferences, etc.).

Learn everything you can about your target market. The more you know, the more you'll be able to create marketing (and services) that will resonate with them. Therefore, one of the first questions I ask a prospect is who they're targeting.

Years ago, I was at a networking event. I struck up a conversation with an acquaintance and asked about her business. Who was she

Chapter 10: Maverick Advisor Rule 10

targeting? Her response made me laugh and cringe at the same time. "Oh... anyone with a checkbook!"

That is not targeting a market. Instead, it's the equivalent of throwing Jell-O at the wall to see what sticks. At another business expo, I came across a new cybersecurity company. I asked them the same question. Their response? They knew they could help any company. Really? Any company?

Here's the truth: it is extremely difficult to market to "any company." Think about it. Would it matter to you if a company just sent you a message that said, "Our soda is better than anyone else's. Try it and see for yourself!"

Or would it make more of an impact if the company instead said this:

> *In a world of fake news and fake flavors, our delicious Berry-Cherrie Health Tonic is a breath of fresh air. No additives. No sugar. Just pure, honest ingredients for those who live life honestly.*

There are several concepts in that statement which would resonate with a specific demographic. More consumers want food and drink without chemicals or complex additives. Millennials like anything with a "natural" look or vibe. They also are drawn to anything that has a "life purpose" message.

The point is to take the service you offer and "dress it up" to match the market you want to attract. If you are targeting tradesmen, offer clear, no-frills type of language. If you want to reach those with a net worth of $5 million and above, then you'd need to use marketing that reflected the image of an exclusive boutique-style service with a high level of personal attention.

If you already have a good idea of the type of target market you want to serve, the next step is to discover what they want. Although Steve Jobs famously said his job was to figure out what his customer wanted before they knew, there is still much value in checking in with your market.

Client Surveys

If you already have clients that fall into your target market, then you have a great opportunity to learn even more about them. There are two different approaches to getting more information about your target market. First, you can quickly and easily send surveys to your clients. Second (and I prefer this method), you can interview your clients.

Clients appreciate it when they're asked about the quality of service they receive. Even if you might be reluctant to hear what they say, it will be a learning experience even if there are concerns on the part of your client.

Another quick story: Years ago, when I first started my copywriting business, I decided to target golf courses as potential clients. I like golf and figured I could help golf courses get more business with marketing tactics that would encourage repeat business.

I spoke to one golf course owner on the phone. His course was the closest one to me and I called to see if I could ask him a few questions about his marketing. One of the questions I asked was if he ever asked his customers to fill out a customer service survey.

His answer surprised me. "Sure, I've used surveys," he said. "But I don't really care for them. The patrons then expect me to do something about what they commented about." I almost was at a loss for words.

It was tempting to say, "What do you think a survey is for? It's to understand what your customers want and what's most important to them so you can serve them better."

Chapter 10: Maverick Advisor Rule 10

I cannot stress this enough. There really isn't any better way to learn how your clients view your services until you ask them. It is the #1 way to improve your business.

Surveys don't have to be complicated, either. There are several ways to conduct a survey. You could send questions on a printed piece of paper and mail it to your clients along with a self-addressed stamped envelope to make responding easy.

Or you could feature an online survey where you could instantly view the results. I've used SurveyMonkey, which is a free online survey service. You can create a survey of up to ten questions. The benefit of using an online service is you can get specific statistics on the results, such as how many men vs. women filled out the survey, which survey takers filled out a comment question, and more.

Also, because the survey provides more anonymity, the client will often share information they may not share if they were filling out a printed questionnaire. A few tips for creating your survey:

Keep it short. You don't want to ask your busy client to take more than 10 minutes to fill out a survey. Anything longer is an imposition on their time and unless you've bribed them with a gift card, it's better to avoid lengthy questionnaires.

Keep a tight rein on the questions. Only ask questions that will serve your purpose. You don't want to sift through a bunch of useless information and neither does your client want his or her time wasted. Save time and get a better response by only asking the questions that are essential to your goal.

Begin with open-ended questions. Open-ended questions are usually the type of questions that will reveal the most information. A good survey is a mix of multiple choice, yes/no questions, and open-ended questions. When you ask an open-ended question and allow your client to write their response, you'll discover insights that might surprise you. Even better, you'll quickly see a pattern if there is either something positive or negative going on with your service. If several people comment on the way their phone calls are treated, for instance, you can instantly address it with your staff.

Here are several other online survey services you can use:

- Typeform
- Google Forms
- Client Heartbeat
- Zoho Survey
- Survey Gizmo
- Survey Planet

Google Forms is the only free online survey tool that provides free skip logic, which is a great feature. Skip logic is a feature that changes what question or page a respondent sees next based on how they answer the current question.

A shorter way to gather marketing intelligence is by adding a feedback form to your website. Your website designer can help design or install one. It's a simple box on a webpage that generally asks, "How are we doing?" or "How can we improve this page for you?"

Make sure you or a staff person knows where those answers are collected so you can view them on a consistent basis. It does you no good to collect information but never review it.

Interviews

Interviews are my favorite because you can follow up with more questions if a client reveals something you didn't expect. Other survey methods will give you a certain level of information. However, with

Chapter 10: Maverick Advisor Rule 10

an interview, you'll be able to notice what a client is passionate about. The more emotion in a response, the more you know it's a good "hot button" topic.

Interviewing a client allows you to dig deeper into the classic question, "What keeps you up at night?" Start to pay close attention when you discern your client answers an aspect of that question with passion in his or her voice.

As mentioned above, when a client answers a question with passion, you'll be able to investigate the topic better by following up with more questions. This can only happen in accordance with a real-time conversation.

If you don't feel comfortable asking your clients questions, you can always bring in an objective third-party who can do it for you. I've conducted customer interviews for my clients to write a case study. Sometimes a client will feel more comfortable talking to someone not directly connected with the business. Whether you conduct the interview or a staff member or another outside vendor—you can expect to get interesting results.

Even inviting a client to lunch and asking questions can be helpful. Ask if it's okay to take notes and start writing. Your clients are the best source for insights regarding how you deliver your service. They'll appreciate the fact you want their opinion and that you desire to improve their experience.

Ultimately, researching your audience is the #1 secret to great marketing. I left the best nugget for last! **If you want your marketing to have the greatest impact, the best decision you can make is to study your market thoroughly.**

The more information you can gather about your prospects, the better chance you'll have to create the kind of marketing that will hook

Chapter 10: Maverick Advisor Rule 10

them. That is the goal of marketing—to connect to your audience. Yes, it takes time, but it is well worth it.

Bland marketing is forgettable. You'll blend in with your competition and cause the buyer to revert to price-shopping. Allow your marketing to do what it was built to do: shine a beautiful light on your unique offerings so your audience chooses *you*.

Remember to get your FREE book bonuses at www.TheMaverickAdvisor.com/bonuses

Afterword

It's always a challenge to end a book like this because I know there is a lot I didn't cover. I don't want to overwhelm you, but instead, I do hope I presented some ideas on how to market your practice better in an increasingly competitive marketplace.

As I mentioned toward the beginning of the book, marketing is re-inventing itself faster every year. Each year, there are new players in the marketing technology world, social media, marketing automation and more. The role of Chief Marketing Officer is becoming more complex as the person struggles to keep up with the fast pace of innovation.

However, I have found in my 30+ years of experience that it isn't necessary to keep up with the latest and greatest new marketing tool. You can market your practice well by adhering to the marketing basics mentioned in this book.

John Wanamaker (1838—1922) was a successful United States merchant and religious, civic, and political figure, considered by some to be a champion of advertising and a "pioneer in marketing." He opened one of the first and most successful department stores in the United States (John Wanamaker & Co.), which grew to 16 stores and eventually became part of Macy's.

Afterword

He coined the famous marketing phrase "Half the money I spend on advertising is wasted; the trouble is I don't know which half."

Many marketers chuckle when they hear the quote, nodding their heads in agreement. Discovering "what works" is the life-long goal of anyone involved with marketing. However, you won't know until you give your marketing enough time to prove whether a strategy or tactic works or not.

Therefore, I stress to my clients the importance of testing. Give your marketing time to "gel" and then look at the results. Test various marketing tactics for 6 months to 1 year. There are even larger brands that don't give their marketing enough time to perform, often ending a marketing initiative too early.

The truth is your prospect is busy and overwhelmed. They may not notice your newsletter much—at first. But after receiving it for four or five months, something might finally click for them. They may suddenly realize their current firm isn't meeting their needs. Or a new service you offer is just what they've been wanting.

I love marketing because I love to experiment. Not everything I test works, but I always gain insight that otherwise I wouldn't have received. It's important to realize in today's overly marketed world, there is always room for improvement.

As you move forward in developing your own marketing strategy, I hope you realize that ultimately, it's all about the client—and not you. If you continue to focus your marketing efforts on helping your client, and they recognize you're focused on meeting their needs, you'll be further ahead than many of your competitors.

Keep swinging for the fences and enjoy the home runs you make! Without marketing, your business will always be less than what it could be. Your success—and the growth of your business—depend upon you investing your time and resources into your marketing.

Acknowledgements

This book would not have happened without the love and support of a team. First, I want to acknowledge my parents, Anthony, and Josephine Helbling. My late mother bought me those wonderful Golden Books when I was a child and I eagerly devoured them. I officially became a rabid little bookworm.

My father surprised me one Friday by bringing home two grocery bags full of library books. I was eight years old and in heaven as I realized I had the whole weekend to read them. Bliss! Because my parents encouraged my love of reading, it automatically created a love for learning. Without my insatiable curiosity and appetite for new information, I wouldn't have had much to say to you (although my family might dispute that).

I also have deep gratitude for my husband, Mickey, who from the very beginning of our courtship confidently told me I'd likely write a book someday. Throughout the years, he has been a stalwart companion, my biggest fan, and my rock during trying times. It is because of his love and writing experience that I finally stepped forward to write this book. Thank you, my sweet man. We did it.

There are always people who have had an influence upon a writer. For me, my high school newspaper was my first foray into getting published. I then wrote for the University of Cincinnati's campus newspaper. Throughout the years after graduation, I always sought opportunities to write. The desire deepened when I served as a pastoral advisor for the Morningstar School of Ministry in Charlotte, North Carolina. The ministry had a quarterly publication, which featured one of my articles. I remembered working hard on that piece and it gave me a taste for more.

Specifically, I'd like to thank the following who have had a profound influence upon me as a marketer and copywriter: Starr Daubenmire, Aimee Kunau, Steve Roller, Clayton Makepeace, Brian Kurtz, and Ed Gandia. Especially Aimee, who has encouraged me in every way to write this book (and start a podcast... someday). I also am grateful for Starr's laser-sharp criticism regarding my website copy and other creative ideas. Her insights were invaluable. I also am in debt to Maria Polson Veres, who generously gave her time and expertise to edit this book. A creative writing teacher, author, and poet, her sharp eye helped "trim the fat" so the concepts were clearer and more concise.

There are many other copywriting teachers and trainers who have cleared a path for me. Some are no longer with us and others still are. First on that list is Dan Kennedy, who opened my eyes to "Magnetic Marketing" and the concepts of creating customer loyalty.

The others: I stand upon the shoulders of giants. Direct marketers will recognize these names of past legends: Claude Hopkins, John Caples, David Ogilvy, Claude Bedell, Jane Maas, Gary Halbert, and Clayton Makepeace. And the living legends: Gary Bencivenga, John Forde, Robert Bly, John Carlton, Carline Anglade-Cole, Kim Krause-Schwalm, and Marcella Allison. I have learned so much from all of them and continue to implement their wisdom.

Finally, I am incredibly grateful to Salim Omar, CPA, Artie Bernaducci, IAR, Ron Lykins, CPA, and Dan Cuprill, Certified Financial Planner and Wealth Coach. All have not only been great clients but offered me an inside glimpse into the world of accounting

Acknowledgements

and financial planning which allowed me to understand how I could help other professional service providers.

It is said that the teacher learns more than the students. In writing this book, I also have learned a lot. It is my hope that the knowledge I've accumulated over the past three decades has somehow been distilled into a tidy package you can use to grow your business. Marketing continues to evolve as we discover new ways to learn about our audience. However, whether you use the tried and true methods of offline marketing or the newer tech-driven online marketing tactics—just focus and continue to experiment until you find the right solution for you.

Thank you for reading this book. Please let me know your success stories, too. Visit https://www.maryrosemaguire.com/contact-us/ and fill out the form on the Contact Page. I love nothing more than to help business owners create marketing strategies that get results.

And finally, if you are interested in writing your own book but unsure where to start, please consider scheduling a conversation with me. If you're interested in improving your lead generation, attracting high-caliber clients, and getting the kind of publicity that opens doors to new opportunities, publishing your own book can be one of the most powerful marketing tools you'll ever have.

You also know things. And people need what you offer. Sometimes it takes someone from the outside to accurately showcase your inner brilliance. Contact me and we'll see if it's time to finally achieve your own dream of being a published author.

Remember... marketing is an experiment, not a contract written in stone. If you're consistently putting forth an effort, you will eventually discover the marketing strategy that works for you. Implementing a "one and done" solution won't change things. But a willingness to test new approaches, new ideas, and new tactics, will. I'll be cheering you on!

About the Author

Mary Rose "Wildfire" Maguire is the Founder of Star Maker Marketing (formerly Maguire Copywriting) and CMO of Mickey Maguire Photo. Star Maker Marketing offers business owners and thought leaders the opportunity to share their expertise with ghostwriting services and book promotion marketing strategies through multiple channels.

Mary Rose wrote the winning entry for the small business category for the Better Business Bureau's Torch Award for Ethics, which led to local and national publicity for a Columbus cybersecurity company. She has written copy for Tripwire, a leader in cybersecurity (acquired by Belden for $710MM), Trainz (national leader in buying and selling collectible trains), My Patriot Supply, Cylance, an AI-based cybersecurity company (acquired by Blackberry for $1.4 billion), information marketers such as The Healthy Back Institute and Small Biz Lady, and dozens of mid-size companies and small businesses.

Mary Rose is the co-author of *Get Happy, Write Away*, and author of *5 Ways a Single Woman Can Find Love After 40: A Systematic Approach for the Older Single Woman Who Wants to Make Every Minute Count While Enjoying Life*. She has written 6 marketing eBooks on copywriting, content marketing, and email marketing,

About the Author

and 2 information marketing products focused on finding "The Big Idea" and how to create and optimize a landing page.

Mary Rose has appeared on 610 WTVN, WTTE FOX28, in *The Columbus Dispatch* and *The Barefoot Writer*. She has been featured as a guest on the following podcasts, **The High-Income Business Writing Podcast with Ed Gandia, Business Breakthrough with Estie Rand,** and **Holistic Helper Reconnect with Beverly Sartain.** She has spoken at the Ohio Society for CPAs' annual conference, the CPA Marketing Genius semi-annual event, Upper Arlington Lifelong Learning Center, the Columbus Metropolitan Library, Ohio Web Leaders, the Dublin Entrepreneurial Center, the Marysville Entrepreneurial Center, and for other local business groups.

Mary Rose has a B.A. in Communication Art from the University of Cincinnati and studied graphic design at the University of Dayton. She is an alumnus of the MorningStar School of Ministry and was the Pastoral Advisor/Administrator for three years at the school.

She is a past member of the National Speakers Association and Toastmasters. Mary Rose is also a student of American Writers and Artists, Inc. and a member of Nos Lumine, a Catholic Leaders business group. She is an avid reader, amateur photographer, and inventive cook. When not focused on marketing, she enjoys visiting outdoor locations with her husband, Mickey, drinking in nature and capturing as much of it as possible with her Pentax DSLR K-50.

Made in the USA
Columbia, SC
12 February 2021